GENEALOGY OF THE

HOLT FAMILIES

FROM SCOTLAND TO VIRGINIA TO TENNESSEE TO MISSOURI AND SEVERAL MIDWEST STATES

INCLUDING THE 230 MARRIAGES THE REV. JAMES MADISON HOLT RECORDED IN NORTH EAST MISSOURI, 1830-1904

PAUL LAWRENCE HOLT, JR.

ISBN: 978-1-948638-53-1

Library of Congress number:

For questions and inquiries, please contact the author:

Paul L. Holt, Jr.
9497 Twin Valley Ct.
West Chester, OH 45241

p.l.holt26@gmail.com

(937) 242-7052

CONTENTS

Forward .... *ix*

The Ancient History of the Holt Family Name in England 1

Holtes of Greslehurst, Lancaster, England 1

Pedigree of the English Families of Holte of Astson Hall 5

The Holt Families of Rochdale, Lancashire 11

    Early Descendants of the Holt Family 12

Rev. James Madison Holt 19

    Children of Rev. James Madison Holt and Elizabeth Luckett — First Family 22

    History of the 44th Virginia Volunteer Infantry 25

Alphabetical Listing of Names from Marriage Register 29

Marriage Register of Rev. James Madison Holt 35

Charles Madison Holt 57

Harry Whitney Holt 61

Paul Lawrence Holt Sr. 67

Paul Lawrence Holt Jr. 79

Paul Clayton Holt 111

James Lawrence Holt 117

HOLT

THE HOLT FAMILY AND ITS COAT OF ARMS

MOTTO: *"Exaltavit humiles"* (He exalted the humble)

ARMS: Azure, two bars or, in chief a crosse formée fitchée of the last.

CREST: A squirrel sejant or, holding a hazel branch, slipped and fruchted all proper.

This coat of arms, with crest and motto is recorded as authentic for Nicholas Holt, who came from Warwickshire, England on the ship "James", and settled in Newberry, Mass. in the year 1635. His family traces back to the Holts of Aston Hall, Warwickshire, who were descended from John atte Holt {i.e. John living at Holt), during the reign of Edward II.

These arms are also shown for the Holts of Erdington Hall, Warwickshire, indicating common ancestry. Sir Thomas Holt, of the Aston Hall line was Sheriff of Warwickshire in 1597, and was created a baronet in 1612.

The surname Holt refers to the locality of origin, meaning, "at the holt", a grove por wood. Towns of this name are to be found in a number of counties in England. Early English records, including the "Hundred Rolls" of 1273 list this family name. At this early date, however, the name is usually prefixed De, De la, Del, or LeHolt. It also appears as Holte.

In 1644, Nicholas Holt, with nine other settlers removed to what is now Andover, Mass. He was evidently a surveyor, or engineer, for various records refer to roads which he was commissioned to lay out. He was married to Elizabeth Short in England, and she bore him four sons and four daughters. She died at Andover in 1656, and he married (second) Hannah Rolfe. They had one son and one daughter.

By the end of the seventeenth century branches of this family were to be found in a number of places in Massachusetts and New Hampshire. Today, branches of this old and distinguished family can be found in every state in the Union, and they are well represented in the arts, sciences and professions, as well as the world of commerce.

To those desiring more detailed information concerning this family, the following references are suggested:

- Crozier's "General Armory", 1904 edition.
- Burke's "General Armory", 1878 edition.
- "Americana", Vol. 19, pub. 1925 by American Historical Society, Inc.

Published by Moms Bros., deVillers & Co. Inc., 254 West 34th Street, New York I, N.Y.

FORWARD

On July 6, 1980 the southwest was devastated by intense heat, which affected many of the elder citizens of Dallas, Texas. Harry Whitney Holt (1892–1980) was one of the six who perished in this heat wave. Among his personal effects, was found a small leather booklet, which belonged to his Grandfather, Rev. James Madison Holt. This booklet recorded two hundred and thirty marriages witnessed and identified by Rev. Holt during his ministry from 1842 to 1900. Most of these parties were from Lewis, Knox, Clark and Marion County, Missouri (Northeast Missouri).

It is the hope of the author that the history of many Missouri families may be advanced by the publication of this book. Great care was taken to duplicate the exact spelling of each name, however it should be noted that the manuscript was hand written and subject to errors.

The author's biography is longer than most because he experienced an insider view of General Motor's Buick Division at the zenith of its influence in the automobile world. In the year 1955, General Motors captured almost 53% of total automobile domestic sales. Buick Division took third place in domestic sales. In 1986, Buick sold over a million units, an all time high, but did not capture third place in domestic sales. The domestic market in 1955 was just over seven million five hundred thousand units. The domestic market in 1986 more than doubled that figure. In the 1990s, domestic sales exploded, reaching a high of seventeen million units, with foreign cars taking about forty percent of the market.

The author wishes to acknowledge the help of Larry Heisey, whose computer talent made the document possible. Also to the hundreds of people that answered the authors letters and inquires over the past forty years.

THE ANCIENT HISTORY OF THE HOLT FAMILY NAME IN ENGLAND

Using manuscripts as the Doomsday Book, the Ragman Rolls, the Curia Regis Rolls, The Pipe Rolls, the Hearth Rolls, parish registers, baptismals, tax records, and available ancient documents and found the first record of the name Holte in Lancashire, England, well before the Norman Conquest and the arrival of Duke William at Hastings in 1066 A.D.

The Saxon race gave birth to many English surnames, including the surname Holte. The Saxons were invited to England by ancient Britons in the 5th century. They were a race of fair skinned people living along the Rhine valley as far north east as Denmark. This immigration was led by Generals Hengist and Horsa. The Saxons settled in the county of Kent, on the south east coast of England. Gradually they probed north and westward, and during the next four hundred years forced the Ancient

Britons back into Wales and Cornwall in the west, Cumberland to the north. The Angles, on the other hand, occupied the eastern coast, the south folk in the Suffolk, north folk in Norfolk.

Under Saxon rule, England prospered under a series of Kings, the last of which was Harold. In 1066, the Norman invasion from France occurred and their victory at the Battle of Hastings. After this, many of the vanquished Saxon landowners forfeited their land to Duke William and his invading Norman rule. Others moved northward to the midlands of Lancashire and Yorkshire, away from Norman oppression. The English family name, Holte, first recorded in Lancashire about 1190, when

Hugo Holte was lord of the manor of his estate. By the 13th Century, Holtes had branched to Stubley, Bishham Hall, Shevington, and Ince in that same shire.

HOLTES OF GRESLEHURST, LANCASTER, ENGLAND

This information was obtained from the library, College of William and Mary, Williamsburg, Early dates were not available, but it does relate to the progression of this family.

Ralph Holte Esq. Of Greslehurst, married Ellen, daughter and heir of John Sumpter, Esq. Their marriage produced John, the heir, and Allen of Bury in Suffolk county. Allen married Agnes Searl and had issue John, who married Ann, daughter of Richard Coote, Esq. Blomorton county of Norfolk, they had a son named John who married a daughter of William Roper, Esq. of Cheshire, and two daughters: Elizabeth, who married Anthony Butler of Cheshire, and Anne who married Henry Collin, Esq. of Norwich. It is not clear if the three sons, Robert, William, and James were an issue of Ralph or of the latter John.

James Holte Esq. of Greslehurst married Isabel, daughter and heir of John Abraham, gentleman of Abraham county of Lancaster. They had at issue Ralph Holte, Esq. who married Anne, daughter of John Langley, gent. of Agercroft County, Lancaster. They produced Thomas, the heir and Robert.

Thomas Holte is listed as a Knight (not to be confused with Aston Hall family — at least no connection has been established). This Sir Thomas married Dorothy, daughter of Sir Ralph Langford, Knight, and by her had issue: Francis, the heir, Ralph and Richard.

Francis Holte Esq. of Greslehurst (living in 1567) married Ellen, daughter of Sir John Holcroft Knight. This marriage produced six daughters, and six sons: Thomas of Greslehurst, who married a daughter of _____ Littleton, Esq., Richard, Francis, Ralph, John and Edmond.

John Holte, Esq. married daughter of _____ Scofield, of Woodsold county, Lancaster, and had an only son, John.

John Holte Esq. married a daughter of _____ Coy, Esq. county Bucks. Had a large family, none listed except Rowland.

Rowland Holte was a London merchant who married Mary daughter of Thomas Buckner, Esq. of London and died in 1634. Mary and Rowland had at issue John and Mary, who died in infancy

Sir Thomas, son of Francis above, was a sergeant at law, and was Knighted April 16, 1699. He married Susan, daughter of John Peacock, Esq. of Cumner county of Berks, and died 1686. Susan died in 1700, leaving their two daughters: Mary who married Edward lemen Esq. and Susan, plus two sons, John and Rowland.

Sir John Holte born at Thame, December 30, 1642. He was lord Chief Justice of the King's Bench in 1696. He died 1710 at Redgrave. He married Anne, sister of Sir John Cropley, Bartister, no children. Left his estate to his brother, Rowland. On Rowland's death, the Estate was to pass to Rowland's eldest son, John or John's male issue. In default of such, the estate was to go to Rowland's second son, Thomas, or his male issue. In default to Rowland's third son Rowland or male issue. In default to Rowland's fourth son, Henry Holte, or male heir, or to other sons of brother Rowland. If Rowland had no other male heirs, the Estate was to go to Edward Leman son of Sir John's sister Leman or his male heirs. In default to John Levett, eldest son of Sir John's sister Levett or in default to Richard Levett. The Estate remains unsettled.

Rowland Holte Esq. born 1632. He was made chief prothonotary of the King's bench in 1690. He died February 11, 1719. Married Prisca, daughter of Augustus Ballow of Norwich. He was a merchant. He and Prisca had John born 1693, who married Lady Jane Wharton, sister of Philip, Duke of Warton on July 3, 1723. Lady Jane later married Robert Coke Esq. of Longford County, Derby. They had a son who died in infancy. Rowland's second son was Thomas Holte of Reading County, Berks. He married Lucy, daughter of John Kynvett, Esq. of Norwich on May 23, 1721. Thomas died November 6,1728. Thomas and Lucy had an issue: Thomas, baptized 1723, snd died 1726. Pisca died in infancy. Lucie died young. Elizabeth, baptized 1726, and married Thomas Strangways Esq. of Greys Inn, London. Thomas died in 1778. Thomas and Elizabeth had a daughter and heir, Louisa, who married Richard Strangways of Wells.

Rowland Holte, youngest son of Redgrave, born 1698 and died July 25,1739, leaving issue of: Rowland Holte, Esq. of Red-

grave. M.P. for Suffolk. Died unmarried July 12,1786.

Thomas Holte of Redgrave, succeeded his brother Rowland. He married Frances, daughter of _____ Porson, Esq. of Parndon County, Essex. Thomas died August 21,1799, age 68. Another brother, Charles, no information. A daughter, Lucinda, who married Thomas Wilson. A daughter, Mary, who married Lloyd Esq., later married Thomas Earl of Haddington on October 28,1750. Mary died 1785. A daughter, Priscillla, no information. A daughter, Charlotte, who died unmarried in 1785, and Jane, who married Sir Thomas Head and died 1803.

Redgrove was an estate of the lordships, given to the Abbot of Bury by the Earl of East Angles, who fell in 1016 at the battle of Assendium Essex, with Canute the Dane. After the dissolution, it was granted by Henry VIII in the last year of his reign to Thomas Darcy, from whom it soon came into the ownership of the family of Bacons. Sir Nicholas Bacon, lord keeper of the seals to Queen Elizabeth, made it his seat, and his descendant, Sir Nicholas Bacon, was created by King James I, the premier Baronet of England on June 22, 1611. One of his successors sold the estate late in the 17th century, to Sir John Holte. Lord Chief Justice in whose hands it continued until it became, by marriage the property of Admiral Wilson.

Redgrove was built of stone by an Abbot of Bury and belonged to the Prelate of that monastery. The house was rebuilt around 1770 by Roland Holte, Esq., who also embellished that park at an expense of 30,000 pounds. The house is a spacious structure of brick, the center is adorned with a pediment, supported by four large columns. The park is wooded, and has a fine lake in the front of the house.

Judge Joseph Holt born Jan. 6, 1807 — Died Aug. 1, 1894. Born in Breckenridge county, Kentucky, was the oldest of the six children of John Holt and Elanor K. Stephens. He was the grandson of Joseph Holt and a descendant of John Holte who was a son of Rowland Holte. Judge Joseph Holt was Postmaster General, Secretary of War during the Civil War. He also served as Judge Advocate General. He was the Judge who sentenced Mrs. Surratt to be hanged at the trial of the assignation of President Lincoln. Judge Holt was married twice, first to Mary Harrison, and second to Margaret Wickliffe, daughter of Charles A. Wickliffe. No children from either marriage. Judge Holt lost his eyesight and died shortly thereafter, in his home on the corner of New Jersey Ave. and C Street, S.E., Washington D.C.

PEDIGREE OF THE ENGLISH FAMILIES OF HOLTE OF ASTSON HALL

Several years ago, I traveled to Fort Wayne, Indiana to visit the Genealogy Section of their local Library. I found an interesting book titled *History of the Holtes of Aston* by Alfred Davidson. Printed by Birmingham Press, East Evert 66, New Street, London dated 1854. I made a copy of the first thirteen pages, and filled it away. It wasn't until several years later that I discovered Aston Hall was close to Rochdale, Lancashire, England. Also Randall Holte was born in Prestbury Parish, in the County Palatine of Chester in 1607, a short distance from Lancahire.

Several years later, I found that a distant relative, Robert Holte, was born in 1605 at Rochdale, Lancashire, England. He married Dorothy Heywood on Dec. 15, 1625 in the cathedral, Manchester. I wrote to the Church and ask if their records contained any records of earlier Holte families. I was advised that baptism records were available, but no family histories.

While I am not able to confirm the connections with our American family, there exist a strong possibility that our family is an extension of what follows. Also Randall Holte, the first Holt to come to America in 1620, may also be a relative.

Henry del Holte, whose history and birthplace is not known, died about 1295. Exact date was not given. From this, his birth data should be around 1250. The only son was stated as follows. Hugh del Holte — Married Maud daughter of Sir Henry del Erdington, Baron of Erdington. He died 1322 leaving a son.

John atte Holte — Married Alice, daughter of Sir George Castell, formerly lords of Withybrook, in the county of Warwick. He died about the year 1330. He left sons, Simon, and Thomas.

Simon del Holte — Married Albreda. In 1331 purchased the park and manor of Neehells. Thomas Holte - Married Margaret, daughter of John de Collesley.

John atte Holt "the elder' — was living in 1348. Married to Maude Grimsarowe. Had two sons, John and Walter.

John atte Holte — Married Agnes, daughter of William Durvassal of Spernall. In 1365 he purchased the manor of Duddeston from John de Grimsarowe, for forty marks. In 1367, his mother conveyed to him the manor of Aston. He passed away leaving no children and was succeeded by his Uncle Walter.

Walter atte Holte — Married Margery, daughter of Sir William Bagot of Baginton. In 1376-7 he served as Escheator for the Counties of Warwick and Leieester. He also served as the Commissioner in Warwickshire for collecting taxes, granted by Parliament to the King. He and his wife settled in the manor of Aston. When Walter passed, his wife Margery willed the estate to John of Gaunt, Duke of Lancaster, Sir William Bagot, of Baginton, and other persons of quality. A dispute occurred and John Drayton petition the House of Lords in 1393 to turn the manor to Richard and Elizabeth Lonches. When the inquest was assembled, Sir William Bagot, with a large company and threatened the Sheriff and petitioners, thus keeping the manor in the hands of the Holte family. Walter had three sons; John, Simon, and William.

John Holte — styled of Yardley. Little is known. John had his residence on a plot of ground; contiguous to the churchyard of Yardley. A moat encircled the plot of ground on which was formerly a mansion house. He had one son, Andomar, who succeeded him.

Audomar Holte — succeeded to the estate of Aston Hall on the death of his father. The King challenged the legal title to the prop-

erty, as son and heir of John, Duke of Lancaster. He had possessed the manor only three years, when Sir William Bagot, considered his claim equal to that of the King Henry IV, and advanced a claim to the property. In 1403, Sir William Holte was elected Knight of his shire, being received into royal favour, claimed the estate. Both parties referred the matter to arbitration of Edward, Duke of York, and Richard Beauchamp, Earl of Warwick. Sir William Bagot, the plaintive, died in 1407. After the lapse of time, Audomar asserted his claim and in 1431 recovered the manor in the course of law, before the Judges of the King's Bench.

William Holte — who is styled of Stanford in 1401. He held the office of Sheriff of Worcestershire in 1422. He died about 1440, and John his nephew, was restored the rightful owner of the manor of Aston.

John Holte — His first wife was Margaret, daughter of Sir Richard Delabere, Knight of Kynardsley, Herefordshire.ln 1438 he was appointed Escheator for Warwickshire and leicestershire. In 1460, on the rebellion of Richard Neville, Earl of Warwick, John Holte was made Ranger of Sutton Chase. His second wife was Joyce Raynford, who he married before 1470. He had two children. Elizabeth, who married John Rudgeley of Wigginton, and a son, William.

William Holte Esq. — He married Mary, daughter of William Cumberiord, Esq., of Cumberiord in the County of Stafford. They had three sons, William, who succeeded him, John and Thomas. Thomas was a member of the Guild of Knowle in 1498. William was a merchant of the Staple. Besides his sons, he had six daughters; Alice, Joan, Anne, Margaret, Christian and Elizabeth.

William Holte, Esq. — Married Joanna, daughter of Adam Knight, Esq., of Shrewsbury. She was alive in 1511. He had a family of four sons. Thomas, his successor, Mark, John, and Nicholas; and seven daughters, Elizabeth, married to Weston; Margaret married to Stanley of Derbyshire; Anne, married to Piers of Warwick; Frances married to Forster of Shropshire; Ellen married to Perman; Winefrid to Thomas Hawkins of Warwick; and Margery to Nicholls. William lies buried in the north aisle of Aston Church, under an altar tomb, on which rests his life-sized effigy. He died in 1514.

Thomas Holte — He was a "learned lawyer" and Justice of North Wales in the reign of Henry VIII. He married Margery, elder of the seven daughters of William Willington of Barcheston, a wealthy merchant of the Staple. The Justice lies buried in the north aisle of Aston Church, by the side of his father. His monument being made of brass, laid in the floor. It contains portraitures of himself and his wife. An inscription, below list Thomas deceased the 23rd day of March 1545. The justice had a son, Edward, and is supposed to have another son John or Joseph, who had a son Barnaby, who was baptized at Aston on September 13, 1579. A daughter, Isabella, baptized September 2, 1580. His estate was considerable and amounted to £270, 6s, 2d., and was exhibited before proper authorities at Sutton Coldfield on April 4, 1546.

Edward Holte — succeeded his father was born 1541. Since he was only four when his father expired, he was placed in guardianship to Sir Ambrose Cave, who married his mother, Margery. Edward, when he became of age, married Dorothy, daughter of John Ferrers, Esq., of Tamworth Castle. The Ferrers family was one of the noblest that sprang from the Norman chiefs of the Conquest. Edward was Justice of the Peace for Warwickshire and served the office of High Sheriff for the county in 1583. By letter patent dated July 1, 1573, Queen Elizabeth gave Edward the rectory of Aston for a period of twenty-one years, after the expiration of the sixty-year lease granted to Philip Hobley, dated March 18, 1531.

In the will of his grandfather, William Willington, Edward Holte inherited considerable property. Edward died Feb. 3, 1592. His wife

Dorothy died Dec. 20, 1594. They are buried with their ancestors at Aston. Their monument being affixed to the wall near his grandfather. The upper part of the monument is encircled with a semicircular arch, flanked by plain round pillars with Corinthian capitals. Over the pediment is a shield with the armorial of the Holte family. Beneath the shield is the motto "Exaltavit humiles" (He has exalted the humble).

In Edward's will, he leaves £500 each to his two daughters, Margaret and Mary, to his son Francis, the parsonage of Shenstone, Staffordshire. To his son Robert, property in Weston in Arden, near Bulkington, Warwickshire, an desires his executors to put this son as an apprentice to a merchant in London and when he reaches the age of twenty-one to make an "advancement" for him. Edward left three sons and six daughters. Thomas, the eldest son that succeeded him to the estate, Francis, and Robert. The six daughters were: Anne who married Edward Easte, Esq.; Lucy, who married John Hugford, Esq.; Catharine, who married Humphrey Wyrley Esq. of Handsworth; Mary, who married George Smyth, Esq. of Wootton, Warwickshire; Dorothy and Margaret, who died unmarried. To his Eldest son Thomas, he leaves the remainder of the estate, who was to come into possession of attaining his twenty-second year.

Sir Thomas Holte — was born in 1571. He resided in Aston Hall for sixty-two years. At the age of twenty-eight (1599) he served the office of Sheriff for the county. In April 1603, he was a member of a deputation to welcome King James to England. On the 18th of the same month, he was designated as Cheshire and received the honor of Knighthood. On Nov. 25, 1612, he was further advanced to the dignity of a Baronet. The reason for this rapid advance, was the province of Ulster was in a state of rebellion, and King James needed to raise military forces to suppress the rebellion. Any gentleman, who was descended from a father or grandfather who bore arms in the defense of England, and was willing to support "thirty foot soldiers in the Kings Army at the rate of 8d. Sterling per day" for a period of three years, for a total of £1,095; would be granted a Baronetey. A year after the creation of this order, ninety-three gentlemen obtained this dignity.

Sir Thomas had a family of fifteen children. The first son, George, (1598-1611), the second son, Robert, died young. The third son, Edward, was born 1600. At the age of fifteen, he entered Hertford College, Oxford. It is not known if he earned a degree. He married Elizabeth, elder daughter of Dr. King, Bishop of London at College in 1634. Sir Thomas was not in favor of this marriage.

On June 21, 1599, Sir Thomas purchased the rectory of Aston, which had been granted to his father. He began remodeling and expanding the mansion and moved into the structure in May 1631, even though it was not finished until April 1635.

Sir Thomas was held in high regard by the court and by King Charles. He was named Ambassador to the Court of Spain, but on the plea of advanced age, he declined this office. On October 16th and 17th, 1642, King Charles with his Army was marching from Shrewsbury to relieve Banbury Castle, staid at Aston manor as a guest of the loyal old Baronet.

On the Sunday after the royal visit, the Battle of Edge Hill was fought, and Edward Holte was wounded. He recovered and was engaged in the defense of Oxford in August 1643. In the discharge of his duties, Edward contracted a fever and he died on the 28th of August 1643. The sentiments of Sir Thomas regarding Edward's marriage to Elizabeth did not change.

In his will, dated 1650, he bequeathed £100 to his grandson, Robert, and to his other grandson, John, the estates at Pipe and Erdington. He died Dec. 14, 1654.

THE HOLT FAMILIES
OF ROCHDALE, LANCASHIRE

Tracing family history of early members of our family is not easy, since records are not available or incomplete. The records from Robert Holte, born 1605 have been recorded and certified. My daughter, Mary Holt Bubier, obtained the records from 1275 to 1605 from Ancestry.com. I am sure there are more family members in each generation. This shows the head of each family, and some information on each member.

John De Holte — Born 1275 and died 1347 in Rochdale, Lancashire, England. He married Maud _____. She died in 1339. Their son was:

Hugh De Holte who was born 1335 and died in 1420 in Heywood, Lancashire. He married Maud Ashworth who was born in 1338 and died in1420. She was from Rushworth Hall. There also was a Hugh Del Holte from the Aston Hall family, who married Maud Erdington. I thought at first there was a connection, but notice the difference: Our family middle name was De and the Aston family was Del. our son was

Sir Richard Holte born in 1420 and died in 1465 in Rochdale. He married Marga-ret Cheetham, born in 1420 and died 1478. Their second son was Christopher Holte, born 1440 and died 1517. Their third son was Geoffery Holte, born 1445 and died 1541.

Oliver Holte, their third son, was born 1455 and died 1522. He married Constance Rushton, who died in 1510. They produced a son.

Henry Holte born 1480 and died 1544. He married Mary Ashetono. No dates for birth or death. Their son was:

Richard Holte born 1500 and died 1597 in Rochdale. Richard married Alice Bynum born 1505 and died 1556. Their son was:

Roger Holte born 1525 and died 1575. He married Sarah Priestley who had no dates for birth or death. Two sons were recorded.

Nicholas Holte born 1532 and died 1590 in Swthabts, England

JAMES HOLTE born 1560 and died in 1599. James married Elizabeth Stanclish who was born 1549. They produced

Robert Holte born 1605.

From this point on, records were produced by produced by Paul L. Holt, Jr.

EARLY DESCENDANTS OF THE HOLT FAMILY

Robert Holte was born about 1605 in Rochdale, Lancashire, England. He married Dorothy Heywood on December 19, 1625 at the Manchester Cathedral, according to the Boyd's Marriage Index. His death was recorded in July 1661, in St. Mary's County, Maryland. The Marriage records for the Manchester Cathedral in Rochdale were not available, however the Baptism records were. These records were very basic and printed in Latin. They reflect one hundred and fifty-one Holte baptism from 1582 to 1607.

Since Robert and Dorothy were married in 1625, it follows that their children would follow after that date. It would appear that Robert II was born before his baptism on October 22 1626. Richard was baptized on November 30 1628. Dorothy (daughter) was baptized on January 31, 1630. James was baptized on February 13, 1631. Elizabeth was baptized September 1, 1633. Elizabeth was buried in Rochdale, Lancashire in 1633, so she died in infancy. There were six other baptisms beginning in 1635 with Robert Holte as the father, but these could have been another Robert Holte.

Richard Holte, second son, was born in November 1628. He was a Cavalier, loyal to King Charles 1st as was his older brother. A Cavalier is similar to our National Guard. Trained in military matters and on call from the King. Cromwell was gaining power in England and was a threat to all who were loyal to the King. I believe Robert Sr. fled England with his wife and family and brought them to America. Since Jamestown, Virginia was the largest settlement, that must have been their destination, however they arrived in Maryland sometime in 1646. When they arrived, the family dropped the "e" from their last name.

Jamestown was the first settlement established in the "'new world" in 1607, and became the center of commerce and land expansion. The Indian uprising of 1622 effectively reduced the size of the settlements by two-thirds. Responding to this threat, the Governor formed a voluntary militia to protect Jamestown and surrounding settlements. With their service as Cavaliers, both Robert and Richard were certain to be included. Land records issued show 500 acres on the Chickahmoiny River at the head of Checqneroes Creek were issued to Robert Holt and Richard Bell on March 2, 1638. On July 20, 1640 Robert Holt was awarded 700 acres on the easterly side of Chickahominy River for transportation of 14 persons to Virginia.

Robert Holt was listed as among the Justices present at the James City County Court on April 27, 1647. Robert Holt represented James City County in the House of Burgesses in 1655-1656 and again in 1667. Richard was also involved in several land purchases, surrounding Jamestown.

Indians were constantly plundering the livestock and grain of the farmers in the outlining areas. Fanners had requested protection from the Governor, but none was provided. Under the leadership of James Bacon, the farmers marched on Jamestown to demand protection. The militia was called, under the command of Lt. Col. Robert Holt.[11] This took place in 1676, One hundred years before the Revolution. It was called "Bacon's Rebellion" The meeting turned violent and Jamestown was almost destroyed by fire. Rather than rebuild Jamestown, the center of government was moved inland, to higher ground and renamed Williamsburg. Four men were tried for treason and hung. Among them was Col. Thomas Hansford, who was the brother of Elizabeth Hansford, who married Randall Holt II (son of Randall Holt — the first Holt to arrive in Jamestown in 1620). Not related to Robert, at least this has not been confirmed. Both Randall and Robert were from the same general area in England. Randall was Palatine County, Chester, England and Robert was Rochdale, Lanchishire.

Richard's first wife was Elizabeth Hudson. They were married about 1667. She died in 1682. To this union was born Richard II in 1668 in So. Farnham Parrish, Essex County, Virginia. Richard II married Mary _____. A daughter, Elizabeth, birth and death not recorded, but she was married twice. First to John Brasher who died in 1712, and her second husband, William Hudson Jr. who died in 1729. Their second son, Robert Holt, birth not recorded, but died in 1698. Robert was married to Elinor Smith. Third son was David, birth not recorded, but died cc 1734, in Prince Anne County, Virginia.

Richard's second wife was Margaret Plunkett. They were married cc 1683. Her birth was not recorded. She died cc 1698. Two sons were born of this union, William, born 1684. He died April 4, 1734 in Essex County. Second son, Plunkett Harraway, born 1689 and died cc1785. Both William and Plunkett were placed with their half brother David, when Margaret died and Richard had previously past away cc 1693.

Plunkett Harraway Holt was born in Essex County, Virginia married Elizabeth _____, date not recorded, but assumed to be cc 1689. Plunkett and Elizabeth had a family, but only one son was listed in their will, Plunkett Harraway Holt II was born cc 1726.

Plunkett II married Ann _____ date not recorded, but assumed to be cc 1745. A large family followed. James' birth and death not known. He married Eleanor Ellander. Robert birth 1774, died 1834. He married Sarah _____ in Cambell County, Virginia. Josiah's birth 1776, death not known. He married Sary Jackson Oct. 19, 1786 in Prince Edward County, Virginia.

The only daughter; Sally, birth and death not known. She married Ludwell Foster, Dec. 27, 1787, in Prince Edward County. George, birth 1765, death in 1840. Married Mary Gilliam in 1810 in Cambell County, VA. Jesse born 1758, died 1802. He married Mary Ward Feb. 12, 1798 in Prince Edward County, VA. Leonard's birth and death not known.

He married Judith Mason in Cambell County, VA in 1810. John's birth and death not known. He married Henietta Smith on Jan. 20, 1800. David Lee Holt, born cc 1763 and died cc 1811. Married Elizabeth McGehee in 1802. Last son, Asa Holt, birth and death unknown. Married Susanna Mason. Held Cook County, TN land grant #23858 in 1841.

David Lee Holt was one of Plunkett H. Holt's nine sons. The 1785 Head of Families of Prince Edward County, VA. lists David with nine white souls, which would mean seven children (or possible relatives) living with David and his wife. Since Richard Shane and Jacob W. Holt were born after 1785, we assume David had nine children. David was a Deacon of the Sailor Creek Church, Rice, VA. in 1802. He owned land in Prince Edward County, so we assume he also was a farmer. The Sailor Creek Church was destroyed by a cyclone in 1832. On August 15, 1857, Pisgah Church (Rice) was formed at Union, and in 1881 moved to their present building at Rice's Station. Pisgah is thus the lineal descendent of the Sailor Creek Church.

Richard S. Holt was born in 1787 in Prince Edward County, VA. He married Nancy Deshazer on September 30, 1806. On November 26, 1812, Richard sold 48 acres of land that he had inherited from his father for the sum of $264.

At this time, Richard and Nancy had three children. Their first child was a daughter, born in 1807. Their second child was Henry J. Holt, born 1811 and named after Richard's father-in-law, Henry J. Deshazer. Third child was John Deshazer Holt, born 1813. All three of the children were born in Amelia County, Richard Shay died in 1853.

Henry J. Desazer was almost like a father to Richard. Henry had been a Revolutionary War soldier. His pension file can be found in the court records in Harrodsburg, KY. He was called into service in Prince Edward

14

County in 1779, into a company commanded by Capt. Devereaux Garnet. He was in the battles of King's Mountain and the Cowpens also Blackstock Ford on Tyson Creek.

He traveled to North and South Carolinas as well as Savanna, GA, when attached to the 3rd Georgia Regiment under Col. Ray (or Rhea). He was attached to Col. Hugh's company for three months. Captured in the spring of 1781, and was a prisoner for three months.

He appeared before Mercer County, KY court on August 10, 1832 to apply for his pension. His age at that time was 72, and was a resident of Glenn's Creek in Mercer County. He died in August 1843, and was buried on Green Johnson Farm. He left heirs: James Deshazer, Jane (Deshazer) Leonard, Abram Deshazer, Nancy Ann (Deshazer) Holt, Jesse. Deshazer, and William Deshazer.

The text below came from four sheets copied from court records in Harrodsburg, Kentucky, by Marie Menaugh Sandusky, Sept. 5, 1962, Harrodsburg, Kentucky. It was taken from HISTORICAL RECORDS OF HARRODS-BURG (MERCER COUNTY) formerly known as Old Crab Orchard, Lincoln County, Stanlord, Kentucky, and are recorded in Part I, Sections 65 and 66, pages 38 and 39 of said volume.

Deshasure:		316, 362
Deshazer:	Henry (Father-in-law of Richard Shay Holt), Georgia	
Deshazure:		South Carolina

State of Kentucky: Mercer County, Aug. 10, 1832. Appeared in open Court in Mercer County. He was a resident of Glenn's Creek in said County, aged 72, says he was born in Prince Edward County, Va. Where he resided at the time he was called into service in May 1779. He enlisted in said County, with John House or Shouse, under Capt. Devenveny Garret, for three years, and my Company marched through North and South Carolina to Savannah, Georgia, where I was attached to the said Georgia Regiment commanded by Col. Ray or Rhea and Lt. Col. Elbert and I was in the Battle of Savannah and at Brier Creek, where we had to retreat.

When Savannah was taken, General News was Commander and he was succeeded by General Green from the time I enlisted until /Savannah was taken. And to Augusta, when we were reinforced, we returned in pursuit of the British, who had followed us, and at Brier Creek, while making a bridge across Brier Creek. The British crossed in or near and we had to retreat, and I had to swim Brier Creek

and the Savannah River, and again rendez-voused at Mulberry Grove in South Carolina. And again returned to Augusta, where I was discharged at the expiration of my time.

On my way home at Salida River, I was taken prisoner by the Tories, who stripped and took my Discharge. I was detained prisoner about one week when I made my escape, and in the neighborhood of a Col. Branham, I volunteered in Capt. Hugh's company of said Branham's Regiment of the S.C. Militia, who was employed in supplying the Tories and in the spring of 1781, I was again taken by the Tories on Brown's Creek in S.C. and in 86 Jail, and in which place I was confined when Gen. Green's Army besieged it., and after Genl. Green's retreat.

After being confined in jail for months, I was taken out for the purpose of being put onboard a prison ship, but on my way to Stone, I again made my escape. After we had been fed on wheat in the shed, and I again got back to Gen. Green's Army on the Waturn River and again returned to my company of

?Capt. Hugh's where I continued until Lord Conwallis was taken and I was discharged, having served 3 years in said Georgia Regiment of the Continental Line and 2 years in the Militia Service of South Carolina.

Further states he knows of no man except Benjamin Warford by whom I can prove any of my service, as there are no persons that I know of from Georgia who live in Kentucky and I am too old to search after them.

I further state that while I was in Col. Branham's Regiment, I joined Gen. Morgan and was engaged in the Battle of Cowpens, where we bust (?) Col. Tarlton. This battle was in January, and the fall before I was with Col. Branham at the Battle of King's Mountain. When Col. Campbell, Col. Cleveland, Col. Shelby and Col. Williams all had a regiment and were present with us. And I was also at Blacklocks Ford on Tyger River where we had a fight with Col. Tarlton. At this time, I was under Capt. Hughes, which various engagements I have omitted in my previous statement.

(Jan. 17, 1761)

Pg. 2 of copy from *HISTORICAL RECORDS OF HARRODSBURG (MERCER COUNTY), KY*, re: Henry Deshazer

Anderson County, Kentucky. This day, Benjamin Wardord, an old Revolutionary War soldier, comes before me, a Justice of the Pease, aforesaid, and being first sworn according to law, doth on his oath declare that I am well acquainted with Henry Deshasure, a Revolutionary War soldier, who is now before me. I knew him in S.C. when he was a solder in the 3rd Georgia Regiment in 1779. We both were young and we volunteered in the same Company and Regiment.

Capt. Hugh's Company and Col. Branham's Regiment and we were together at the Battle of King's Mountain and at Battle of the Cowpens under Gen. Morgan and at Blackstoocks's Ford on Tyger Creek. I have heard the statement of the said Disharm Road and I know he was in the service of his Country in the manner he has detailed.

I was not with him the whole time, yet I know he as out as he lived in the same section of the country, and I believe his details are correct. I was sometimes in other Regiments. I was with Sumpter at Brier Creek and the said Deshasure was with

Col. Branham in the whole of said Disharms Services. I have actual knowledge of more than 2 years because I was with him, either in the same Regiment or in one Company at the Battle he has detailed.

Henry died Aug. 1843, Mercer County, KY.

August 6, 1962

From Marie M. Sandusky,
PO Box 16, Burgin, Ky.

I am enclosing copy of affidavits for proof of service of Henry Deshazer's service in Rev. War. His service was approved and he was granted a pension. His name is on markers here (DAR, etc.) as one of the soldiers buried in Mercer County. Examination of numerous deeds here show his wife was Elizabeth _____? She died only a few months before her husband, Henry. He left four heirs*, as deeds show. Three sons: James, William, Jesse. The other may have been a daughter (or possibly another son). Neither Henry nor Elizabeth left wills. Williams was Admr. For both estates, but the Invtv. Apprsmt & Sale Bills revealed little in way of proof of heirs.

If you need further records and proof of name, I notice there was a suit filed in the Circuit Court. It was a friendly suit of the heirs in order to make proper settlement. It would name all heirs, and most often give much information helpful in genealogy. If you wish me to do this, and make copies of all marriages of children recorded here, I will do so for $10.

* All second wife's children

18

REV. JAMES MADISON HOLT

Born: January 19, 1818, Log Cabin near Buck Creek, Lincoln County, Kentucky

Married: Elizabeth Luckett, Oct. 31, 1839
Second marriage: Margaret A. Mobley, Feb. 22, 1855

Died: September 20, 1904, LaBelle, Lewis County, Missouri

Interment: La Belle Cemetery, Lot 27, Section 5, La Belle, Missouri

The fourth child, third son of Richard and Nancy (Deshazer) Holt was born in a log cabin on the farm home, near Buck Creek in Lincoln County, Kentucky. He spent his boyhood until the age of seven in the wild wilderness of this frontier land. His family then moved to Williamson County, Tennessee. At the age of thirteen, he began to assist the schoolteachers with teaching the lower grades. In 1834, the family moved to Marion County, Missouri, six miles north of Palmyra, Missouri.

The last school he taught was at La Grange, Lewis County, Missouri.

On October 31, 1839, he married Elizabeth Luckett. To this union were born five children, John Thomas Holt (1841–1862), James Richard Holt (1843-died between 1889 and 1904), Edward Livingston Holt (1845-1936), Frank Shay Holt (1847–1929), and Mary A. Holt (Palmer) (1849–unknown) His first companion having preceded him in death, he was again united in marriage to Margaret A. Mobley on February 22, 1855. To

Rev. James Madison Holt with Margaret, his second wife.

this union were born four children, Charles Madison Holt (1858–1930), Fannie Elizabeth Holt (1860–1947), Katie L. Holt (Berry) (1864–unknown) and Albert Holt, who died in infancy.

In the 1850s, Missouri was known as a "Swing State." Which meant it was divided between Slavery and Freedom. Those who supported slavery saw it as a way to end their way of life. Those who opposed slavery pointed to the Declaration of Independence and "All men are created equal."

Rev. Holt's father, Richard had owned slaves in Virginia and supported slavery. There must have been many harsh discus-

sions over this matter in the Rev. Holt's household. Two of his sons from his first marriage enlisted in the Confederate Army. Records from the Museum of the Confederacy, Richmond. VA, confirm that John T. Holt enlisted Sept. 1, 1862, Company A, Steen's Regiment, Missouri Volunteers. He was promoted to 3rd Corporal on November 10, 1862. He was wounded in the battle of Prairie Grove, Arkansas, on December 7,1862 and died five days later. James R. Holt, second son (first marriage) of Rev. James M. Holt, enlisted in the Confederate Army on June 8, 1861 at Amelia Court House, VA, as a Private in Company H of the 44th Regiment, Virginia Infantry. He was wounded in the Battle of Port Republic, VA on June 9, 1861.

It would appear that he had no training, and was rushed into combat. Recovering from an abdominal wound, he was detailed to drive supply wagons. On Oct 31, 1864, he was transferred to Company I 44th Virginia Infantry, and was made a teamster on ordnance trains. He was taken Prisoner of War, belonging to the Army of Northern, Virginia, which surrendered on April 9, 1865 at Appomattox Court House, Virginia. He was paroled on April 10, and returned to Missouri.

Edward Livingston Holt, third son of Rev. Holt's first marriage, entered the Union Army at seventeen. Because he was underage, he was made a 'Drummer'. He was not allowed to carry a weapon, and his main activity was to recover wounded soldiers after battle. He survived the war and married Jane Carr Donald on April 13, 1875. He died on May 2, 1936. Frank S. Holt, the forth son, first marriage, was born 1847, married Eva Ross on October 18,1876, moved to Oklahoma Territory and died Nov. 15, 1929 in Kay County, Oklahoma. The fifth child was a daughter, Mary A. Holt, born 1849. She married Palmer. The last marriage preformed by Rev Holt was on Jan. 10, 1900 when he married his Granddaughter, Lula R. Palmer to Denny L. Kinney, both of Quincy, IL.

Approximately 1840, at the age of twenty-two, Rev. Holt was baptized and united with the Bethel Baptist Church in Marion County. Later he moved to Lewis County and joined the Gilead Baptist Church. In 1840, he felt called to GOD, and was ordained to the ministry by the Gilead Church, Lewis County, Missouri. Most of his ministerial labors were performed in Lewis, Clark, Knox, Scotland" Marion, and Shelby Counties. He served as pastor in the following churches: Gilead, Dover, Ten Mile, LaGrange, Monticello, Wyaconda, South Fork, Providence, Liberty, Mt. Pleasant, Canton, Emerson, Sand Hill, Lewistown, Bee Ridge, Knox City, Newark, Mt. Salem, and North River. Of these churches, he served Dover, Liberty, and Newark, for eigh-

The last picture of Rev. James Madison Holt.

teen years each. He organized three churches: Canton, Monticello, and Mt. Salem.

On October 25, 1844, The Wyaconda United Baptist Association was formed by the union of eight churches. It was an outgrowth of the Salt River Baptist Association and the Bethel Association. James M. Holt, then a layman of the Bear Creek Church, served as a messenger to this organization meeting. He was appointed one of five men to serve on the Constitution and By-Laws Committee.

He was elected Moderator of the Wyaconda Baptist Association on September 7,1860. And served in that capacity for sixteen terms (1860-1870 and 1878–1884). This association founded the Hannibal-LaGrange College, later to be called LaGrange College. He was deeply interested in advancing education and spent much time and energy, securing financial assistance.

Rev. Holt was a Whig, during the days of that political party. Later he became a Democrat. He served as Postmaster of Newark in 1887. He was a member of the Masonic Lodge, and had taken all the degrees in the Blue Lodge, Chapter, and Council.

The legacy he leaves is his Marriage Ledger of almost two hundred and marriages which two hundred and thirty are recorded in this publication. (see index) These marriages were performed from February 1830 through January 1900. It is hoped the remainder of these marriages can be recovered, as the ageing process has made them illegible.

CHILDREN OF REV. JAMES MADISON HOLT AND ELIZABETH LUCKETT — FIRST FAMILY

JOHN THOMAS HOLT

The first son of this family was born in 1841. He did not appear to have been married, as no records were found. John enlisted in the Confederate Army on Sept. 1, 1862 He was assigned to Company A, l0th Regiment Missouri Infantry. He was promoted to 3rd Corporal on Nov. 1, 1862. He was wounded on Dec. 7, 1862 in the Battle of Prairie Grove, Arkansas and died five days later. I believe he was reburied on Jan. 1, 1867 in Plot 101, Confederate Cemetery, Alton Illinois, Madison County, which is just east of Quincy, IL, where his parents lived.

JAMES R. HOLT

The second son of this family was born in 1843. He returned to visit relatives in Amelia Court House, V A and enlisted in the Confederate Army on June 8, 1861 at the age of 17. He was assigned to Company H, 44th Regiment Virginia Infantry. It appeared that he was rushed into combat without training, as he was wounded in the Battle of Port Republic, Virginia on June 9, 1861 On Dec. 31, 1861, he was detailed to drive wagons. He was transferred to Company I the 44th Virginia Infantry on Oct.31, 1864 and made a Team-Master on Ordnance Train. He was taken Prisoner of War, belonging to the Army of Northern Virginia on April 9, 1865 at Appomattox Court House, VA. He was paroled the following day and returned to Missouri.

EDWARD LIVINGSTON HOLT

The third son of this family was born on October 18, 1845, Lewis County, Missouri. He married Jane Carr Donald on April 13, 1875, in Neelyville, Illinois. He died on May 2 1936, in Los Angles, California. He served in the Civil War as a Union Drummer. Since he was very young he was allowed to only be a Drummer (could not carry firearms). All Drummers were expected to care for the wounded in battle. Descendants of his family are as follows:

WILLIAM ARTHUR HOLT

Born January 15, 1876. He married Lena __ . No record of his death or of his family.

JAMES T. HOLT

Born July 1, 1880. No record of his marriage. He died prior to 1898 in Neelyville, Illinois.

MAUDE J. HOLT

Born February 22,1882. Married George N. Thompson of Ottumwa, Iowa on March 26, 1902. No records of family.

RUTH E. HOLT

Born March 13, 1884. Married Joseph Mahan of Los Angeles, California. Died October 27, 1933 in Los Angeles, CA. Children of Ruth and Joseph are:

JOHN MAHAN

Born March 13, 1910 in Los Angeles. No record of family.

WILLIAM MAHAN

Born in Los Angeles.

ARTHUR EUGENE MAHAN

Born February 7, 1916 in Los Angeles. Married Thelma Yeats. From this marriage was born:

DEBORAH RUTH MAHAN

Born August 21, 1950. Married John A. Rupp on March 1, 1969. She kindly gave me the history of Edward L. Holt's family. Her children are:

JANINE MARIE RUPP

Born February 13, 1970. Married Cortis D. Orgvski.

DAVIS SCOTT RUPP

Born April 1, 1971 Married Staci on April 4, 1992.

TIFFANY ELLEN RUPP

Born November 3, 1972 Married Mark Graca on April 30, 1992.

JESSIE B. HOLT

The fifth child of Edward Holt - Born January 22, 1886. Married Clark Fry

GUY DONALD HOLT

The sixth and last child of Edward Holt was born September 1, 1888. He married Winnefred Lindell. Died on March 4 1995. His children were:

MARIE ELOISE HOLT

Born June 16,1925 in Spokane, WA.

DONALD EUGENE HOLT

Born February 25, 1927 in Spokane, WA

RICHARD LYLE HOLT

Born August 17, 1931 in Spokane, WA.

JAYNETA JANE HOLT

Born October 2, 1937 in Spokane, W A.

FRANK S. HOLT

The fourth child of Rev. Holt was born in 1887.He married Eva Ross on October 18, 1876 They moved to Oklahoma City, OK., where he died. They had one child, a daughter.

HISTORY OF THE 44TH VIRGINIA VOLUNTEER INFANTRY

The units that would eventually comprise the 44th Regiment of the Virginia Infantry were recruited from the central Virginia. The 10 companies were accepted into the Virginia state forces on June 14, 1861, in Richmond. They were sworn into Confederate service around July 1, 1861. William Campbell Scott was selected as the first colonel of the regiment. He would serve the regiment until his resignation on December 31, 1862. "Often in the forefront of action, General Richard S. Ewell credited the 44th Virginia for turning the tide in the battle of Port Republic on June 9, 1862." (K. C. Ruffner, 44th Virginia Infantry) At Port Republic, the 44th Virginia was usually in the thickest of the fighting in every engagement.

The 44th was assigned to Edward Johnson's Army of the Northwest, which was later incorporated into Stonewall Jackson's fabled Army of the Valley. The regiment would ever afterwards be associated with Jackson and the Second Corps, Army of Northern Virginia.

The regiment was virtually annihilated at Spotsylvania in May 1864. 158 men, the colonel, major, and 16 captains and lieutenants were captured when Federals overran their exposed position in the Mule Shoe. The regiment suffered only 1 man killed and 2 wounded in the brief encounter. Their flag was seized by a member of the 64th New York. The remnants of the units were consolidated into one company and surrendered 17 officers and men, torn by 4 years of war, at Appomattox. These men truly deserve to be called veterans. Few units ever saw more intense actions than the 44th Virginia Infantry.

The companies of the 44th Virginia Infantry were:

Company A: Appomattox Invincibles hailed from Appomattox County, enlisting on April 26, 1861, and originally was commanded by James E. Robertson. This company was removed from the 44th Virginia in March 1862 to form Company C of the 20th Battalion Virginia Heavy Artillery.

Company B: Boyd Rifles were recruited from Goochland County. Their commander was William Lacy. They enlisted en masse on April 1st.

Company C: Travis Rifles hailed from Buckingham County and enlisted with their commander Thomas Buckner on June 6th.

Company D: Ambler Grays were a conglomerate from 4 different counties, Louisa, Fluvanna, Goochland, and Hanover. They were sworn into service June 8th under the command of Joseph Shelton.

Company E: Richmond Zouaves was the only company not from a rural locality. They came from the capital city of Richmond. They enlisted June 10th and were commanded by Edward McDonnell, Jr. This company withdrew from the regiment and became Company E of the 19th Battalion Virginia Heavy Artillery. However, they were ordered to return to the 44th Virginia in late February 1863.

Company F: Fluvanna Hornets hailed from Fluvanna County. They were commanded by Thomas Weisiger and entered service on May 20th.

Company G: Randolph Guard resided in the counties of Prince Edward and Cumberland.

They enlisted June 8th with Norvell Cobb commanding.

Company H: Amelia Minutemen from Amelia County, also enlisted on June 8th, with Thomas Coleman as company commander.

Company I: Mossingford Rifles hailed from Charlotte County. William H. Marshall commanded them and they entered service on May 8th.

Company K: Fluvanna Guards also hailed from Fluvanna County. Under the command of David Anderson, they enlisted on June 11th.

Sources: Ruffner, Kevin C., 44th Virginia Infantry. Lynchburg: H. E. Howard, 1987 Early, Jubal A. Memoirs — http://www.geocities.com/CapitolHill/Parliament/3347/

44TH VIRGINIA INFANTRY

The 44th Virginia Volunteer Infantry Regiment was an infantry regiment raised in Virginia for service in the Confederate States Anny during the American Civil War. It fought mostly with the Army of Northern Virginia.

The 44th Virginia was organized in June 1861, with men from Richmond and Farmville, and Appomattox, Buckingham, Louisa, Goochland, Amelia, Fluvanna, and Hanover counties.

The unit fought at Rich Mountain, in Lee's Cheat Mountain Campaign, and was active in Jackson's Valley operations. During March, 1862, it was reduced to nine companies as Company A was transferred to the artillery. The 44th served in General Early's, J.R. Jones', and W. Terry's Brigade, Army of Northern Virginia. It was involved in many engagements from the Seven Days' Battles to Cold Harbor, then continued the fight with

Early in the Shenandoah Valley and around Appomattox.

The regiment reported 5 wounded at Greenbrier River, had 2 killed and 17 wounded at McDowell, and lost 15 killed and 38 wounded at Cross Keys and Port Republic. It sustained 15 casualties at Fredericksburg and 71 at Chancellorsville, and of the 227 engaged at Gettysburg more than twenty percent were disabled. Only 1 officer and 12 men surrendered in April, 1865.

The field officers were Colonels Norvell Cobb and William C. Scott; Lieutenant Colonels Thomas R. Buckner, James L Hubard, A.C. Jones; and Major David W. Anderson.

References: This article incorporates public domain material from the United States Government document "Civil War Soldiers and Sailors System", National Park Service. (http://www.civilwar.nps.gov/cwssiregiments.cfm) Retrieved from Wikipedia.com

44TH VIRGINIA VOLUNTEER INFANTRY REGIMENT

Flag of Virginia, 1861

Active	June 1861 – April 1865
Disbanded	April 1865
Country	Confederacy
Allegiance	Confederate States of America
Role	Infantry
Engagements	American Civil War: Battle of Rich Mountain-Battle of Cheat Mountain-Jackson's Valley Campaign-Seven Days' Battles-Second Battle of Bull Run-Battle of Antietam-Battle of Fredericksburg-Battle of Chancellorsville-Battle of Gettysburg-Battle of Cold Harbor-Siege of Petersburg-Valley Campaigns of 1864—Appomattox Campaign
Disbanded:	April 1865

James Madison learned at an early age the importance of eduction. He learned to read and write at the age of 10 and began to act as a teacher to lower classes in school. This was noticed by the Baptist Churches he attended in William County, Tennessee, and when the family moved to Palmyra, Missourir in 1834, he was appointed as a messenger of his Baptist Church. This permitted him to attend the churches who were members of the "Salt River Baptist Association." Later, this group was included in the formation of the "Wyconda Baptist Association." James M. Holt became the secretary of this organization. This accounts for the gap in his marriage book from 1839 to 1859. (All marriages performed after page 11 in his book were performed by him.)

As a messenger of the Salt River Baptist Association, he was responsible for keeping membership records of all churches. Church records were used in the first 11 pages of his marriage manual. He issued Marriage Certificates to those who had not received them previously (see photo). He signed them as a Recorder, and the Pastor signed as the Deputy.

ALPHABETICAL LISTING OF NAMES FROM THE
MARRIAGE REGISTER

NAME	PAGE NUMBER	NAME	PAGE NUMBER
ABELL, Sallie E.	35	BISE, William R.	10
ABLETT, Iney	43	BISHOP, George W.	31
ADAMS. Franklin	21	BISLER, Nanina A.	40
ADA.MS, James M.	17	BLAIR, Susie S.	43
ADKINSON, William R.	2	BLAND, Joseph P.	18
ALDERTON, James W.	24	BOARD, A. L.	18
ALDERTON, Mary C.	21	BOMER, Margaret A.	11
ALLEN, Rebecca	1	BONDUSANT, Sarah F.	36
ALLEN, Williamson G.	8	BOON, Emily R.	9
ANDERSON, Hattie	28	BOOM. John William	39
ANDERSON, Joseph T.	23	BOURN, Joseph A.	39
ANDERSON, Willis E.	44	BOURN, Michael	40
ASBURY, Davis R.	2	BOURN, Ruben R.	46
ASBURY, Capt. Davis R.	19	BOURNE, Abner D.	31
ASKIN, Sarah Ann	2	BOURNE, Hannah	9
ATHEY, Mollie D.	27	BOTTS, Thomas T.	5
BADER. John H.	25	BOWLES, Robbie L.	44
BAIRD, Hatty	12	BRADSHAW, Charles A.	14
BAIRD, John A.	9	BRADSHAW, Emmett	41
BAKER. Davis A.	8	BRADSHAW, Melle	38
BAKER, Erastus D.	8	BREWINGTON, Davis W.	7
BAKER, Lizzie F.	25	BRISCOE, Nancy	5
BAKER, Seth	9	BRISCOE, Sarah E	42
BALL, Bettie C.	19	BROWN, Eliza Jane	21
BALLINGER. Mollie E.	38	BROWNING, Mrs. Jenner Brent F.	47
BALLINGER, Oliver A.	29	BRUMBAUGH, Susie	35
BANE, Agness J.	9	BUCKIEY, William	1
BARCLEY, Sarah S.	7	BUFORD, Nancy A.	16
BARKELEW, Mary A.	25	CAHILL, Mrs. Mary H.	10
BARKLEY, Bettie L.	14	CAIN, Solomon	25
BARNES, Albert	33	CALDWELL, Jane	1
BASHON, Cornnell R.	5	CARPENTER, Mrs. Nancy A.	24
BATE, George A.	12	CARPENTER, Thomas J.	18
BERRY, Callie S.	46	CASON, Alfrida	18
BERRY, Henry S.	42	CATLETT, John W.	14
BERRY, Ida A.	34	CHAPPELL, George A.	7
BERRY, Lucinda E.	35	CHAPPELL, John L.	12
BERRY, Lula E.	42	CHARLTON, John H.	12
BERRY, Ollie K.	32	CHARLTON John. H	12
BILLUPS, Oliver C.	23	CHARLTON, Rafus G.	11

NAME	PAGE NUMBER	NAME	PAGE NUMBER
CHILTON, Medley	31	ERVING, Elizabeth B.	4
CHRISTIAN, Leonidus A.	38	EWALT, Edward T.	30
CLARK, William	10	EWALT, John E.	40
CLEHENT, William C.	32	FARISS, M. B.	6
COBB, Cordelia Ann	9	FARM ER, John C.	24
COBBS, Dorinda	11	FIRESTONE. Re. Simon P.	35
COBBETT, John T.	41	FISHER, Mollis L.	23
COLLINS, Julia L.	23	FISHER, Sarah Jane	3
CONBS, William H.	4	FORD, Jesse	10
CONN, Raphael M.	20	FORHAN, J. W.	28
CONWELL, Dorisilla	15	FORREST, Elizabeth	3
COOTER, Sarah M.	27	FORSEE, John W.	11
CURRIER, Mrs. F. A.	13	FOSSETT, Margaret	18
CRITCHFIELD. Henson	6	FRANCIS, James A.	4
DAGGS, Harriet	4	FRENCH, Aios L.	24
DALE Louise A.	7	FRETWELL. John	14
DAIE. Samuel	3	FULLER, Mary S.	15
DALLAS. Belle	39	GATES, Mary E.	15
DALLAS. Martha	26	GILL, Elizabeth J.	6
DANFORTH, Louisa	13	GLASSCOCK, Annie	45
DANFORTH. Lucinda	12	GLOVER, Emma J.	34
DAUGHTERY, Mary C.	11	GRAVES, Thomas E.	17
DARE, Mrs. Laura A.	45	GREEN, W. A.	44
DAVIS. E. Allen	39	GREEN, William H.	32
DAVIS, Margaret	11	GREGORY, Mary E.	29
DAVIS, Mary	10	GUNN, Charles	34
DAVIS. Mattie E.	19	GUSH, Martin	27
DAVIS. Stephen H.	22	HALDERMAN, James J.	42
DAVIS, William	23	HALDERMAN, Samuel	40
DAY, John A.	38	HALDERMON, William F.	15
DeHAVEN, Marshall L.	30	HALL, James L.	21
DERRNIE. Catharin	2	HALL, William G.	31
DeWEESE, Demerins	29	HALLEY, Winfield S.	30
DEWEY. Elizabeth S.	8	HAMILTON, Samuel	2
DeWITT. Benjamin F.	22	HAMILTON, Anabella	3
DEWITT Mary Fay	20	HAMILTON, Elizabeth	27
DISKERSON, John H.	13	HAMILTON, Priscilla O.	39
DOWNING, Nathan H.	36	HAMILTON, William H.	9
DRAKE, Ida Ruberta	36	HARDMAN, Sarah M.	29
DURRETT, Oscar H.	15	HARILTON, Martha Jo	7
ELLIS, Abraham	24	HAYDEN, Mary L.	42
ELLISON. William J.	23	HAYDON, Sarah A.	44
ERSLEY, Maria	4	HAYDON, Thomas A.	35

NAME	PAGE NUMBER	NAME	PAGE NUMBER
HAYMAN, Samuel H. Dr.	19	KINTZING, Benjamin C.	26
HENDRON, Anderson	34	LACKLAND, Sarah Jane	1
HENTON, Levina D.	12	LACKLAND, Sarah Jane	1
HENTON, Sallie M.	22	LAND, Richard G.	14
HINSON, Charles Ann	28	LAND, Richard G.	14
HOBDAY, Mollie C.	41	LANKFORD, John A.	46
HOBDAY, Sallie	37	LARN, Mary	26
HOBES, Virginia	13	LaRUE, Edwin H.	37
HOHNES, Addie E.	44	LaRUE, Mary E.	15
HOUGES, Sarah E.	30	LaRUE, S. Robert	38
HOUSE, George W.	18	LaRUE, William T.	47
HOUSE, Richard D.	37	LASWELL, Charles	13
HOUTH, Johanna B.	32	LASWELL, Jesse	16
HUME, James R.	24	LASWELL, Mary Ellen	14
HUMPHRY, Nancy Jane	2	LASWELL, William Jr.	33
HUMPHRY, Thomas	3	LaTAG, Mrs. Malinda	39
HUNER, Sarah C.	27	LATHAM, James W.	1
HUNT, Mary C.	8	LAY, James W.	8
HUSSON, John A.	34	LEAR, Charles E.	42
HUTCHINSON, John M.	18	LEAR, Zechaniah T.	36
IRVIN, Rachel S.	12	LEGG, Mattie S.	30
JACKSON, Lutie P.	18	LELAND, Herbert W.	37
JEFFRIES, Rizzrah Ann	3	LESLIR, Clara R.	46
JOB, Ella A.	43	LEWIS, Joseph M.	11
JOB, Franlie D.	20	LILLARD, Davis S.	15
JOB, Jennir J.	40	McCRACKEN, Fannie	41
JOB, Zechanah T.	23	LILLARD, Sarah A.	33
JOHNSON, Abraham	2	LILLY, Mary A.	17
JOHNSON, Albert G.	22	LOCKWOOD, L. R.	17
JOHNSON, James	6	LUCKER, Florence G.	37
JOHNSON, Joseph	1	LYON, Alfred	29
JOHNSON, William R.	7	LYON, Caroline	24
JONES. Clide W.	46	MAGIE, Alexander J.	39
JONES, Lizzie F.	38	MARKS, Anna S.	26
JONES, Sheldon S	3, 26	MARSHALL, Mary A.	34
JORDAN, William H.	10	MARTIN, Ambros	44
KELLY, Minnerva E.	28	MARTIN, Elizabeth L.	4
KELSO, Statera	30	MARTIN, Jeremioh	45
KENNEDY, Mrs. Mary	21	MATTHEWS, Dexter F.	28
KENNEY, E. H.	41	MATTHEWS, George W.	15
KENT, Bellie A.	22	MATTINGLY, Jane D.	2
KESNER, George	3	MATTINGLY, Samuel D.	5
KINNE, Denny L.	47	HAYBERRY, George .A.	22

McCAN, Thompson 3
McCOHN. Erastus W. 10
McCoy, John T. 34
McCRACKEN, Fannie K. 41
McCRACKEN, S. P. 45
McCRACKEN, Sallie B. 42
McCUBBINS, Sylvester 1
McDANIEL, Burch 11
McDANIEL, Mary S. 23
McEUTIRE, Theressa 44
McFEE, Elisha 5
McKENZIE, Sarah A. 31
McREYNOLDS, Leah 16
McREYNOLDS, John S. 45
McVEY, Annie 41
MERRILL, Sarah A. 22
MERRIWETHER, Thomas H. 12
MINER, George R. 28
MINER, John W. 28
MOBLY, Martha E. 10
MOHLFELDT, Alice D. 31
MOFFETT, James M. 25
MONTANE, William H. 35
MONTGOMERY, William H. 21
MOORE, George W. 32
MOORE (or MOON). Joseph A. 4
MOORE, Robert 22
MORRIS, George G. 27
MUIR, George G. 11
MUIR, Richard G 9
MUIR, Susan J. 8
MUIR, William 3
MURPHY, Stephen L. 7
MUSGRIVE, Thomas J. 13
MUSGROVE, Dr. William H. 16
MUSSETTU, Sarah A 14
MYER, Silas. W. 41
MYERS, Eliza J. 31
MYERS, George W. 43
MYERS, Lucy M. 32
MYERS, S. M. 44
NELSON, Elizabeth 21
NELSON, Mary H. 30
NICHOLS, George G 13
NICHOLS, Margaret 14

NICHOLS, Mary J. 20
NICHOLS, Nancy J. 16
NICHOLS. Richard 27
NOEL. Ann Maria 2
NOEL, Mollie H. 28
NOEL, Paulina 1
NULL, Benjamin F. 42
NUNN, Mellie M. 20
NUNN, William A. 21
OLIVER, Augustus 14
PALMER, Henry 17
PALMER. Lulu R. 47
PALMER, Susan J. 27
PARKS, Julia F. 37
PAYTON, Daniel N. 4
PERKINS, John B. 35
PFLUM, Charles B. 36
PICKETT, John 35
PICKETT, Catherine 33
PORTER. Earnest J. 43
PORTER, Adner W. 36
PRICE, Hugh N. 12
PROSSER, Lyda M. 46
PYLES, James B. 45
RAINSEY, Silas M. 25
RAMSEY, James W. 27
RANDOLPH, William H. 38
RAY, Cynthia Jane 6
RAY, James M. 20
RAYBURN, Amanda M. 17
RAYBURN. Nancy M. 25
RAYBURN. Martha Ann 13
RECTOR, Annie B. 37
RICHARDSON, John C. 29
RILEY, Mary Ann 7
RINGER, Lulu B. 38
RISK, Annie E. 17
RISK, Henry C. 25
ROBERTS. Alexander B. 42
ROBINS, Miranda 26
ROBINSON, George 4
RONNER, James G. 33
ROHER, Mary E. 28
ROUSE, Birdie E. 37
ROUTT, Peter L. 26

ROSE, Lannie S. 32
ROSS, Lillian L. 45
ROSS, Guy B. 43
ROSS, Sarah A. 34
ROSS, William B. 34
RUDD, Nattie 45
RUDD. Sylvanus W. 37
SALE, Louisa 7
SAMS, Ida E. 33
SAYERS, Ida 29
SCAGGS, Annie 33
SCOTT, Beatrice M. 31
SCOTT, Martha E. 41
SEBLETT. William K. 7
SHAFER, Ada F. 36
SHIRES, F. Marion 20
SHOUSE. Thomas J 20
SHRISLEY. Jane L. 8
SIMPSON, Hazelline J. 5
SINROCK S. A. M. 23
IHROCK, Mattie E. 32
STIES, Viola N. 38
SLATER, James 39
SLAUGHTER, J. C. 36
SLAUGHTER, Mary E. 31
SLITT, Mary 9
SLOAN. George W. 30
SLOAN, Georgia E. 39
SLOTT Mary 9
SHACK, Julia A. 14
SMITH, Amanda M. 22
SMITH, Dela 36
SMITH, Eliza E. 34
SMITH, Emily G. 7
SMITH, Francis (male) 13
SMITH, Francis (female) 13
SMITH, Fields A. 5
SMITH, H. Clay 17
SMITH, James N. 6
SMITH, Julia 6
SMITH, Hargaret A. 13
SMITH, Martin L. 33
SMITH, Mary A. 16
SMITH, Minriva F. 35
SMITH, Narcissa J. 45

SMITH, Sarah E. 6
SMYSER, Samuel J. 9
SPAULDING, Frank B. 27
SUTER, Martha A. 10
SUTTON, James B. 46
SUTTON, Thomas F. 28
STAFFORD, James J. 19
STAPLES. Adelia F. 19
STEPHENSON, Nancy Ann 5
STEWART, Maggie L. 43
STOKES, E. C. 43
STREET, Issac N. 16
STUART, Ann E. 4
TAYLOR, George W. 41
THOMAS, _____ 26
TOMPSON, Bushrod F. 29
THOMPSON, Elizabeth S. 19
THOMPSON, George W. 6
THOMPSON, Henrietta 12
THOMPSON, James S 16
THOMPSON, Merideth D. 29
THROCKMORTON, J. E. 40
THROCKMORTON, Mrs. Ollie K. 44
THROCKMORTON, Thomas C 32
TODD. Albert R. 43
TRAVIS, William L. 16
TRUE, Jessie I. 46
TULEY, Matild 25
TULEY, Virginia I. 21
TULLEY, Lyda E. 42
TULY, Margaret J. 24
TULY, Mary Ann 24
TURNER, Jake S. 41
TURNER. William H. 38
WAGNER, Sarah C. 19
WAINSCOT, Elizabeth J. 6
WALERMAN, Ruth 20
WALLACE, Susan Ann 5
WALLER, Sarah C. 36
WALTER, Kinrod R. 8
WALTER, Melinda 8
WALTER, Presley K. 21
WALTER, William R. 2
WASHBURN, Annie 40
WATERMAN, Katie 40

WATERMAN. William F. 26
WATKINS, E. G..19
WEBBER, Louisa A. 15
WBBER, Emily R..24
WEKKS, Alva...25
WESTON, Maria Elizabeth 5
WHITE, Madison W. S. 30
WHITE, Margaret 1
WHITE, Mattie S...30
WILLI AMS, Amanda 11
WILLIIAMS, Elizabeth S................................10
WILLI.AMS. William H..................................33
WILLIE, Joseph F. 45
WILSON, Sadia M...33
WILTER, Mary 17

WILSON, Theressa A. 23
WILSON, William 19
WITHERS, Eudora E......................................29
WITHERS, Minriva Ola 39
WITHERS, Narcissa Frances...........................26
WITHERS, Rosia D..40
WITHERS, Sallie...43
WOLFE. Lucretia Ann 16
WOOD, John A...20
WRIGHT, David. P. 37
YORE. B. Ann 22
ZIMMERMAN, Daniel H................................32
ZIMMERMAN, Tihman W..............................31
ZINN, Morrison 40

MARRIAGE REGISTER OF
REV. JAMES MADISON HOLT

	PAGE 1	
Sunday	February 10, 1830	JAMES W. LATHAM and MARGARET WHITE. Both of Lewis Co. Mo.
Thursday	February 14, 1830	JOSEPH JOHNSON married REBECCA ALLEN. Both of Lewis County, Mo.
Sunday	June 16, 1830	SYLVESTER McCUBBINS married JANE CALDWELL. Both of Lewis County, Mo.
Thursday	August 22, 1830	WILLIAM BUCKLEY married SARAH JANE LACKLAND. Both of Lewis County, Mo.
Sunday	September 13, 1830	GEORGE KESNER married PAULINA NOEL. Both of Lewis County, Mo.
	PAGE 2	
Thursday	March 20, 1831	SAMUEL HAMILTON married ANN MARIA NOEL. Both of Lewis County, Mo.
Thursday	April 24. 1831	ABRAHAM JOHNSON married CATHARIN DERRNIE. Both of Marrion County, Mo.
Thursday	August 14, 183l	WILLIAM R. ADKINSON married NANCY JANE MURPHY. Both of Lewis County, Mo.
Thursday	February 19, 1832	DAVIS R. ASBURY married JANE D. MATTINGLY. Both of Lewis County, Mo.
Thursday	March 4, 1832	WILLIAM R. WALTER married SARAH ANN ASKIN. Both of Lewis County, Mo.
	PAGE 3	
Thursday	April 8, 1832	SAMUEL DALE married ELIZABETH FORREST. Both of Lewis County, Mo.
Thursday	November 23, 1832	THOMPSON McCAN of Marrion County. Married SARAH JANE FISHER of Lewis County, Mo.
Thursday	December 16, 1832	WILLIAM MUIR married ANABELLA HAMILTON. Both of Lewis County, Mo.
Thursday	December 23, 1832	SHELDON S. JONES married Ri____ ANN JEFFRIES. Both of Lewis County, Mo.

Sunday	January 2, 1833	THOMAS MURPHRY married FRANCIS SMITH, Both of Lewis County, Mo.

PAGE 4

Tuesday	March 8, 1833	JOSEPH A. MOORE (or MOON) married MARIA EASLEY. Both of Lewis Co. Mo.
Thursday	April 7, 1833	GEORGE ROBINSON married ELIZABETH L. MARTIN. Both of Lewis County, Mo.
Sunday	July 3, 1833	WILLIAH H. COMBS of Scotland Co. t married ELIZABETH B. ERVING of Lewis County, Mo.
Tuesday	October 11, 1833	JAMES A. FRANCIS of Marrion County married ANN E. STUART of Lewis County, Mo.
Thursday	December 29, 1833	DANIEL N. PAYTON married HARRIET DAGGS. Both of Lewis County, Mo.

PAGE 5
Holt was witness to all the wollowing marriages and issued marriage certificates to the happy couples.

Sunday	July 2, 1834	THOMAS T. BOTTS of Lu County, Iowa married NANCY BRISCOE of Lewis County, Mo.
Thursday	October 26, 1834	CORN NELL R. BASHON of Marrion County married SUSAN ANN WALLACE of Lewis County Mo.
Sunday	March 4, 1835	SAHMUEL D. MATTINGLY married HAZELINE SIMPSON. Both of Lewis County, Mo.
Tuesday	April 24, 1835	ELISHA McFEE married MARIA ELIZABETH WESTON. Both of Lewis County, Mo.
Tuesday	May 15, 1835	FIELDS A. SMITH married NANCY ANN STEPHENSON. JI0t.II of Lewis County, Mo.

PAGE 6

Tuesday	October 2, 1835	GEORGE W. THOMPSON married SARAH E. SMITH. Both of Lewis County, Mo.
Thursday	January 10, 1836	JAMES N. SMITH of Aidrian County married ELIZABETH J. WAINSCOT of Lewis County, Mo.

Sunday	August 31, 1836	HENSON CRITCHFIELD married CYNTHIA JANE RAY. Both of Illinois.
Thursday	October 23, 1836	M. B. FARISS married ELIZABETH J. GILL. Both of Lewis County, Mo.
Sunday	November 30, 1836	JAMES JOHNSON married JULIA SMITH: Both of Lewis County, Mo.
PAGE 7		
Thursday	January 1, 1837	STEPHEN L. MURPHY married MARY ANN RILEY. Both of Lewis County, Mo.
Thursday	March 26. 1837	WILLIAM K. SEBLETT married SARAH S. BARCLEY. Both of Lewis County, Mo.
Tuesday	August 25, 1837	WILLIAM R. JOHNSON married LOUISA DALE. Both of Lewis County, Mo.
Thursday	October 8, 1837	DAVIS W. BREWINGTON of Knox County, married EMILY G. SMITH of Clark County. Mo.
Monday	October 12. 1837	GEORGE A. CHAPPELL of Bullit County, Kentucky, married MARTHA J. HARILON of Lewis County, Mo.
PAGE 8		
Thursday	January 7, 1838	DAVID A. BAKER of Lewis County, married ELIZABETH S. DEWEY of Clark County. Mo. Received $ 2.50
Wednesday	February 17, 1838	ERASTUS D. BAKER married JANE L. CHRISLEY. Both of Lewis County, Mo. Received $ 2.50
Tuesday	September 7, 1838	WILLIAHSON G. ALLEN married SUSAN J. MUIR. Both of Lewis County, Mo. Received $ 10.00
Sunday	October 3, 1838	KINROD R. WALTER married MELINDA WALTER. Both of Lewis County, Mo. Received $ 3.00
Sunday	October 10, 1838	JAMES W. LAY married MARY C. HUNT. Both of Lewis County. Mo. Received $5.00

PAGE 9		
Wednesday	November 3, 1838	RICHARD G. MUIR married AGNESS J. BANE. Both of Lewis County, Mo. Received $ 5.00
Thursday	December 16, 1838	SAMUEL J. SMYSER married HANNAH BOURNE. Both of Lewis County, Mo. Received $ 2.00
Wednesday	January 26, 1839	SETH BAKER married EMILY R. BOON. Both of Lewis County. Mo. Received $ 2.00
Tuesday	February 1, 1839	JOHN A. BAIRD married MARY SLITT. Both of Lewis County, Mo. Received $ 2.00
Wednesday	April 15, 1839	WILLIAM H. HAMILTON married CORDELIA ANN COBB. Both of Lewis County, Mo. Received $ 3.00
PAGE 10		
Tuesday	June 7, 1839	ERASTUS W. McCOHN married MARTHA E. MOBLY. Both of Lewis County, Mo. Received $ 2.50
Tuesday	July 26. 1839	WILLIAM CLARK married MARTHA A. SUTER. Both of Lewis County, Mo. Received $ 5.00
Tuesday	August 9, 1839	WILLIAM H. JORDAN married MARY DAVIS. Both of Lewis County, Mo. Received $2.00
Monday	October 17, 1859	WILLIAM R. BISE married ELIZABETH S. WILLIAMS. Both of Lewis County, Mo. Received. $2.00
Sunday	November 13, 1859	JESSE FORD married Mrs. MARY H. CAHILL. Both of Lewis County, Mo. Received $3.00
PAGE 11		
Marriages from this point on were performed by Rev. Holt.		
Tuesday	January 10, 1860	RAFUS G. CHARLTON married DORINDA COBBS. Both of Lewis County, Mo.

Thursday	January 19, 1860	JOHN W. FORSEE married AMANDA WILLIAMS. Both of Lewis County, Mo.
Thursday	February 2, 1860	GEORGE G. MUIR of Lewis County, married MARY C. DAUGHERTY of Clark County, Mo.
Thursday	March 22, 1860	BURCH McDANIEL married MARGARET DAVIS. Both of Lewis County, Mo. Received $5.00
Sunday	May 3, 1860	JOSEPH M. LEWIS married MARGARET A. BOMER. Both of Lewis County, Mo. Received $1.00
PAGE 12		
Thursday	June 28, 1860	GEORGE A. BATE married RACHEL S. IRVIN. Both of Lewis County, Mo. Received $3.00
Thursday	October 4, 1860	JOHN H. CHARLTON married HATTY BAIRD. Both of Lewis County, Mo. Received $1.50
Wednesday	November 28, 1860	HUGH N. PRICE married LUCINDA DANFORTH. Both of Clark County, Mo. Received $2.00
Thursday	May 10, 1861	THOMAS H. MERRIWETHER of Knox County, Married HENRIETTA THOMPSON of Lewis County, Mo. Received $2.00
PAGE 13		
Wednesday	May 16, 1861	GEORGE G. NICHOLS married LOUISA DANFORTH. Both of Clark County, Mo. Received $ 2.50
Thursday	May 30, 1861	THOMAS J. MUSGROVE of Clark County, married MARGARET A. SMITH of Lewis County, Mo.
Thursday	May 30, 1861	JOHN H. DICKERSON of Indiana, married VIRGINIA HOBBS of Lewis County, Mo. Received $2.00

Thursday	November 21, 1861	CHARLES LASWELL married MARTHA ANN RAYBURN. Both of Clark County, Mo. Received $2.00
Thursday	March 12, 1863	FRANCIS SMITH married Mrs. F. A. CURRIER. Both of Clark County, Mo. Received $3.00
PAGE 14		
Wednesday	June 24, 1863	AUGUSTUS OLIVER married Mrs. JULIA A., SMACK. Both of Lewis County, Mo.
Sunday	March 20, 1864	JOHN FRETWELL of Lewis County, Married MARGARET NICHOLS of Clark County, Mo.
Thursday	March 24, 1864	JOHN W. CATLETT married MARY ELLEN LASWELL. Both of Clark County, Mo.
Wednesday	June 8, 1864	CHARLES A. BRADSHAW married BETTIE L. BARKLEY. Both of Lewis County, Mo. Received $10.00
Wednesday	December 28, 1864	RICHARD G. LAND married Mrs. SARAH A. MUSSETTU (?). Both of Lewis County, Mo.
PAGE 15		
Thursday	January 19, 1865	DAVID S. LIILLARD married MARY E. GATES. Both of Lewis County, Mo. Received $10.00
Thursday	January 26, 1865	OSCAR H. DURRETT married MARY E. LaRUE. Both of Lewis County, Mo. Received $4.00
Thursday	March 2, 1865	THOMAS U. GLASSCOCK married LOUISA A. WEBBER. Both of Clark County, Mo. Received $5.00
Monday	March 13, 1865	GEORGE W. MATHEWS of Marrion County, married MARY S. FULLER of Lewis County, Mo. Received $20.00
Sunday	March 19, 1865	WILLIAM F. HALDERMON married OORISILLA CONWELL. Both of Lewis County, Mo.

		PAGE 16
Thursday	March 23, 1865	WILLIAM L. TRAVIS married MARY A. SMITH. Both of Lewis County, Mo. Received $10.00
Tuesday	April 4, 1865	JESSEE LASSWELL of Clark County, married NANCY J. BUFORD of Knox County, Mo. Received $10.00
Tuesday	August 29, 1865	Dr. WILLIAM H. MUSGROVE married LUCRETIA ANN WOLFE. Both of Clark County. Received $10.00
Tuesday	January 1, 1867	ISSAC N. STREET of West Point, Iowa, married NANCY J. NICHOLS of Lewis County, Mo. Received $3.00
Thursday	January 24, 1867	JAMES S. THOMPSON of Lewis County, Married LEAH McREYNOLDS of Knox County, Mo. Received $20.00
		PAGE 17
Thursday	February 28, 1867	THOMAS E. GRAVES married ANNIE E. J. RISK. Both of Lewis County, Mo. Received $11.00
Thursday	July 11, 1867	H. CLAY SMITH married ARTIE J. GILLARD. Both of Lewis County, Mo. Received $10.00
Thursday	August 13, 1867	L. R. LOCKWOOD married MARY WILTER. Both of Lewis County, Mo.
Wednesday	October 23, 1867	HENRY PALMER of Hancock County, Illinois, married AMANDA M. RAYBURN of Clark County, Mo. Received 5.00
Sunday	November 17, 186	JAMES M. ADAMS married MARY A. LILLY. Both of Clark County, Mo. Received $5.00
		PAGE 18
Tuesday	December 24, 1867	JOHN M. HUTCHINSON married ALFRIDA CASON. Both of Lewis County, Mo.

Thursday	January 23, 1868	GEORGE W. HOUSE married A. L. BOARD. Both of Lewis County, Mo. Received $5.00
Thursday	January 23, 1868	THOMAS J. CARPENTER married MARGARET FOSSETT. Both of Lewis County, Mo. Received $3.00
Thursday	February 13, 1868	JOSEPH P. BLAND married LUTIE P. JACKSON. Both of Lewis County, Mo. Received $10.00
PAGE 19		
Thursday	March 19, 1868	WILLIAM WILSON married ELIZABETH S. THOMPSON. Both of Lewis County, Mo. Received $10.00
Tuesday	September 1, 1868	E. G. WATKINS married SARAH C. WAGNER. Both of Lewis County, Mo.
Tuesday	September 15, 1868	Dr. SAMUEL H. HAYMAN married MITTIE E. DAVIS. Both of Lewis County, Mo. Received. $5.00
Thursday	December 17, 1868	CAPT. DAVID R. ASBURY married ADELIA F. STAPLES. Both of Lewis County, Mo. Received $10.00
Thursday	December 24, 1868	JAMES J. STAFFORD married BETTIE C. BALL. Both of Clark County, Mo. Received $5.00
PAGE 20		
Thursday	March 4, 1869	JOHN A. WOOD married MELLIE M. NUNN. Both of Lewis County, Mo. Received $8.00
Tuesday	March 9, 1869	RAPHAEL M. CONN of Pazr (?) County, Virginia, married D. FRANKIE JOB of Lewis County, Mo. Received $8.00
Sunday	March 14, 1869	F. MARION SHIRES married RUTH WALERMAN. Both of Lewis County, Mo. Received $3.00

Thursday	March 18, 1869	JAMES M. RAY married MARY J. NICHOLS. Both of Lewis County, Mo. Received $5.00
Wednesday	September 1, 1869	THOMAS J. SHOUSE married MAY F. DEWITT. Both of Lewis County, Mo. Received $3.00
PAGE 21		
Sunday	September 12, 1869	JAMES L. HALL married ELIZABETH NELSON. Both of Lewis County, Mo. Received $10.00
Wednesday	September 22, 1869	WILLIA MONTGOHERY of Clark County, married Mrs. MARY KENNEDY of Lewis County, Mo. Received $5.00
Thursday	September 30, 1869	PRESLEY K. HALTER married VIRGINIA 1. TULEY. Both of Lewis County, Mo. Received $2.50
Tuesday	November 2, 1869	FRANKLIN ADAMS married MARY C. ALDERTON. Both of Lewis County, Mo. Received $5.00
Thursday	November 11, 1869	WILLIAM A. NUNN married ELIZA JANE BROWN Both of Lewis County, Mo. Received $10.00
PAGE 22		
Tuesday	November 16, 1869	STEPHEN H. DAVIS of Scotland County, married B. ANN YORE of Lewis County, Mo. Received $1.00
Sunday	November 28, 1869	BENJAMIN F. DEWITT married BELLIE A. KENT. Both of Lewis County, Mo. Received $2.00
Wednesday	December 1, 1869	GEORGE A. MAYBERRY married MRS. AMANDA M. SMITH. Both of Lewis County, Mo. Received $15.00
Thursday	January 6, 1870	ROBER.T MOORE married SALLIE M. HENTON. Both of Lewis County, Mo. Received $6.00

Thursday	February 17, 1870	ALBERT G. JOHNSON of Marion County, SARAH A. MERRILL of Lewis County, Mo.
PAGE 23		
Tuesday	March 29, 1870	JOSEPH T. ANDERSON of Hallsville, Wyoming; married MOLLIS L. FISHER of Lewis County, Mo.
Tuesday	April 5, 1870	WILLIAM J. ELLISON of Clark County, married A. HILSON of Lewis County, Mo.
Tuesday	May 3, 1870	WILLIAM DAVTS married S.A.M. Simpson. Both of Canton, Lewis County, Mo. Received. $2.50
Tuesday	September 20, 1870	OLIVER C. HILLUPS married MARY S. McDANIEL. Both of Lewis County, Mo. Received $5.00
Tuesday	September 27, 1870	ZACHAIAH T. JOB married JULIA L. COLLINS. Both of Lewis County, Mo. Received $5.00
PAGE 24		
Thursday	December 8, 1870	AMOS T. FRENCH married Mrs. NANCY A. CARPENTER. Both of Lewis County, Mo. Received $6.
Thursday	February 23, 1871	ABRAHAM ELLIS married CAROLINE LYON. Both of Lewis County, Mo. Received $15.00
Tuesday	February 28, 1871	JOHN C. FARMER married MARY ANN TULY. Both of Lewis County, Mo. Received $5.00
Thursday	March 9, 1871	JAMES R. HUME married EMILY R. WEBER. Both of Clark County, Mo. Received $10 in Gold.
Tuesday	April 4, 1871	JAMES W. ALDERTON married MARGARET J. TULY. Both of Lewis County, Mo. Received $3.00

	PAGE 25	
Wednesday	April 5, 1871	HENRY C. RISK married LIZZIE F. BAKER. Both of Lewis County, Mo. Received $10.00
Thursday	May 25, 1871	SOLOMON CAIN married NANCY M. RAYBURN. Both of Clark County, Mo. Received $5.00
Wednesday	September 13, 1871	SILAS M. RAINSEY married MARY A. BARKELEW. Both of Lewis County, Mo. Received $5.00
Tuesday	November 14, 1871	JOHN H. BADER of Clark County, married MATILDA TULEY of Lewis County, Mo. Received $5.00
Thursday	November 16, 1871	JAMES H. MOFFETT of Lewis County, married Miss ALVA WELLS of Cark County, Mo. Received $5.00
	PAGE 26	
Thursday	November 23, 1971	WILLIAM F. WATERMAN married MIRANDA ROBINS. Both of Lewis County, Mo. Received $5.00
Sunday	December 24, 1871	PETER L. ROUTT married NARCISSA FRANCES WITT. Both of Knox County, Mo. Received $ 5.00
Monday	January 1, 1872	BENJAMIN C. KINTAING of St. Louis. Married Miss MARY LAM of Lewis County. Mo. Received $10.00
Tuesday	February 6, 1872	Mr. THOMAS of Fowler, married ANNA S. MARKS. Both of Lewis County, Mo. Received $5.00
Thursday	March 14, 1872	SHELDEN S. JONES married MARTHA DALLAS. Both of Lewis County, Mo. Received $5.00

	PAGE 27	
Sunday	September 22, 1872	GEORGE G. MORRIS married ELIZABETH HAMILTON. Both of Knox County, Mo. Received $10.00
Wednesday	October 2, 1872	FRANK B. SPANLDING married SARAH M. COOTER. Both of Lewis County, Mo. Received $5.00
Thursday	October 10, 1872	RICHARD NICHOLS married SARAH C. HUNER. Both of Lewis County, Mo. Received $5.00
Tuesday	November 12, 1872	MARTIN GUSH married SUSAN J. PALMER. Both of Marion County, Mo. Received $10.00
Thursday	December 12, 1872	JAMES W. RAMSEY of Lewis County, married MOLLIE ATHEY of Clark County, Mo. Received $10.00
	PAGE 28	
Thursday	January 23, 1873	JOHN W. MINER married MARY E. ROMER. Both of Knox County, Mo. Received $10.00
Thursday	February 13, 1873	THOMAS F. SUTTON married CHARLES ANN HINSON. Both of Lewis County, Mo. Received $5.00
Sunday	March 2, 1873	J. W. FORHAN married MENERVA E. KELLY. Both of Marion County, Mo. Received $5.00
Thursday	September 4, 1873	GEORGE R. MINER married HATTIE ANDERSON. Both of Knox County, Mo. Received $10.00
Thursday	September 11, 1873	DEXTER F. MATHEWS of Knox County, married MOLLIE H. NOEL of Lewis County, Mo. Received $5.00

	PAGE 29	
Thursday	September 11, 1873	OLIVER A. BALLINGER married EUDORA E. WITHERS. Both of Knox County, Mo. Received $5.00
Tuesday	September 16, 1873	MERIDETH D. THOMPSON married MARY E. GREGORY. Both of Lewis County, Mo. Received $5.00
Thursday	January 1, 1874	BUSHROD F. THOMPSON married IDA SAYERS. Both of Lewis County, Mo. Received $5.00
Monday	January 5, 1874	JOHN C. RICHARDSON of Arkansas, Married SARAH IL HARDMAN of Knox County, Mo. Received $5.00
Thursday	January 15, 1874	ALFRED LYON married DEMERINS DeWEESE. Both of Lewis County, Mo. Received $5.00
	PAGE 30	
Tuesday	March 17, 1874	MADISON W.S. WHITE married MARY H. NELSON. Both of Knox County, Mo. Received $5.00
Tuesday	March 17, 1874	MARSHALL L. DeHAVEN of Morgan County, married MATTIE S. WHITE of Knox County, Mo. Received $5.00
Thursday	April 9, 1874	EDWARD T. EWALT married MATTIE S. LEGG. Both of Lewis County, Mo. Received $5.00
Sunday	December 13, 1874	WINFIELD S. HALLEY married STATERA KELSO. Both of Lewis County, Mo. Received $5.00
Tuesday	February 16, 1875	GEORGE H. SLOAN married Mrs. SARAH E. HODGES. Both of Knox County, Mo. Received $5.00

PAGE 31		
Thursday	February 18, 1975	MEDLEY CHILTON married MARY E. SLAUGHTER. Both of Knox County, Mo. Received $10.00
Sunday	April 18, 1875	GEORGE W. BISHOP married SARAH A. McKENZIE. Both of Knox County, Mo. Received $5.00
Thursday	April 22, 1875	WILLIAM G. HALL married BEATRICE M. SCOTT. Both of Knox County, Mo. Received $5.00
Thursday	May 13, 1875	TIHMAN W. ZIMMERMAN married ELIZA J. MYERS. Both of Lewis County, Mo. Received $5.00
Wednesday	May 19, 1875	ABNER D. BOURNE married ALICE D. MOHLFELDT. Both of Lewis County, Mo. Received $5.00
PAGE 32		
Thursday	June 24, 1875	WILLIAM H. GREEN married Mrs. JOHANNA B. HOUTH. Both of Lewis County, Mo. Received $5.00
Sunday	August 15, 1875	DANIEL H. ZIMHERMAN married LUCY M. MYERS. Both of Lewis County, Mo. Received $5.00
Sunday	October 10, 1875	GEORGE W. MOORE married LANNIE S. ROSE. Both of Knox County, Mo. Received $5.00
Wednesday	October 13, 1875	WILLIAM C. CLEMENT of Indiana, married MATTIE E. SINROCK of Knox County, Mo. Received $5.00
Thursday	November 11, 1875	THOMAS C. THROCKMORTON of Lewis County, married OLLIE K. BERRY of Knox County, Mo. Received $5.00

		PAGE 33
Sunday	November 21, 1875	ALBERT BARNES married ANNIE SCAGGS. Both of Knox County, Mo. Received $5.00
Wednesday	December 22, 1875	WILLIAM LASWELL JR. married SARAH A. LILLARD. Both of Lewis County, Mo. Received $10.00
Thursday	December 23, 1875	MARTIN L. SMITH married SADIA M. WILSON. Both of Knox County, Mo. Received $5.00
Sunday	February 6, 1876	WILLIAM H. WILLIAMS married IDA E. SAMS. Both of Knox County, Mo. Received $3.00
Thursday	March 23, 1876	JAMES G. RONNER of Knox County, married CATHERINE PICKETT of Shelby County, Mo. Received $10.00
		PAGE 34
Thursday	March 23, 1876	JOHN A. HUDSON married ELIZA E. SMITH. Both of Knox County, Mo. Received $5.00
Friday	April 14, 1876	CHARLES GUNN married Mrs. MARY A. MARSHALL. Both of Knox County, Mo. Received $5.00
Tuesday	April 18, 1876	JOHN T. McCOY married EMMA J. GLOVER. Both of Knox County, Mo. Received $5.00
Thursday	May 4, 1876	WILLIAM B. ROSS married IDA A. BERRY. Both of Knox County, Mo. Received $3.00
Thursday	June 1, 1876	ANDERSON HENDRON married Mrs. SARAH A. ROSS. Both of Knox County, Mo. Received $5.00

	PAGE 35	
Thursday	August 17, 1876	JOHN PFLUM married MINRIVA F. SMITH. Both of Knox County, Mo. Received $2.50
Sunday	September 3. 1876	JOHN B. PERKINS married MARY E. REAGER. Both of Lewis County, Mo. Received $5.00
Thursday	September 7, 1876	Rev. SIMON P. FIRESTONE married SALLIE E. ABELL. Both of Knox County, Mo. Received $5.00
Thursday	September 7, 1876	THOMAS A. HAYDON married SUSIE BRUMBAUGH. Both of Knox County, Mo.
Thursday	December 15, 1876	WILLIAM H. MONTAGNE married LUCINDA E. BERRY. Both of Knox County, Mo.
	PAGE 36	
Thursday	February 22, 1877	J. C. SLAUGHTER married ADA F. SHAFER. Both of Knox County, Mo. Received $10.00
Wednesday	April 18. 1877	ADNER W. PORTER married SARAH F. BONDUSANT. Both of Lewis County, Mo. Received $5.00
Sunday	September 9, 1877	CHARLES B. PFLUM married SARAH C. WALLER. Both of Knox County, Mo. Received. $1.50
Wednesday	March 6. 1878	ZECHANIAH T. LEAR married DELA SMITH. Both of Knox County, Mo. Received $5.00
Wednesday	April 17, 1878	NATHAN H. DOWNING married IDA RUBERTA DRAKE. Both of Knox County, &. Received $10.00
	PAGE 37	
Wednesday	April 17, 1878	HERBERT W. LELAND married FLORENCE G. LUCKER. Both of Knox County, Mo. Received $5.00

Thursday	December 5, 1878	DAVID P. WRIGHT married BIRDIE E. ROUSE. Both of Lewis County, Mo. Received $3.00
Thursday	December 5, 187	SYLVANUS W. RUDD married ANNIE B RECTOR. Both of Knox County, Mo. Received $2.50
Thursday	December 19, 1878	EDWIN H. LaRUE of Lewis County married SALLIE HOBDAY of Knox County. Mo. Received $5.00
Thursday	October 16, 1879	RICHARD D. HOUSE married JULIA F. PARKS. Both of Knox County. Mo. Received $7.00

PAGE 38

Thursday	January 1, 1880	LEONIDUS A. CHRISTIAN of Marion County, married MOLLIE E. BALLINGER of Knox County, Mo. Received $ 5.00
Tuesday	January 13, 1880	S. ROBERT LaRUE married MELLE BRADSHAW. Both of Lewis County, Mo. Received $7.00
Sunday	January 18, 1880	JOHN A. DAY married VIOLA N. SITES. Both of Lewis County, Mo. Received $5.00
Wednesday	February 11, 1880	WILLIAM H. TURNER married LIZZIE F. JONES. Both of Lewis County, Mo. Received $15.00
Sunday	April 11. 1880	WILLIAM H. RANDOLPH married LULU B. RINGER. Both of Knox County, Mo. Received $10.00

PAGE 39

Thursday	July 29, 1880	E. ALLEN DAVIS of Mama County, Illinois, married BELLE DALLAS of Lewis County. Mo. Received $10.00
Sunday	September 19, 1880	JAMES SLATER married Mrs. MELINDA LATAG. Both of Lewis County, Mo. Received $2.50

Tuesday	October 19, 1880	ALEXANDER J. MAGIE, M.D. married PRISCILLA O. HAMILTON. Both of Knox County, Mo. Received $10.00
Sunday	October 24, 1880	JOHN WILLIAM BOURN of Lewis County, Married GEORGIA E. SLOAN of Knox County, Mo. Received $5.00
Wednesday	September 14, 1881	JOSEPH A. BOURN of Lewis County, married MINRIVA OLA WITHERS of Knox County, Mo. Received $5.00
PAGE 40		
Sunday	December 4, 1881	JOHN E. EWALT of Knox County, married NAURIA (?) A. BIXLER of Lewis County, Mo. Received $5.00
Wednesday	June 28, 1882	MORRISON ZINN married JENNIR J. JOB. Both of Lewis County, Mo. Received $7.00
Wednesday	September 6, 1882	SAMUEL HALDERMAN married ANNIE WASHBURN. Both of Lewis County, Mo. Received $10.00
Thursday	August 30, 1883	J. E. THROCKMORTON of Lewis County, married ROSIA D. WITHERS of Knox County, Mo. Received $5.00
Sunday	September 9, 1883	MICHAEL BOURN married KATIE WATERMAN. Both of Lewis County, Mo. Received $5.00
PAGE 41		
Thursday	December 6, 1883	JAKE S. TURNER of Lewis County, married MOLLIE C. HOBDAY of Knox County. Mo. Received $5.00
Tuesday	September 23, 1884	EMMETT BRADSHAW married FANNIE K. McCRACKEN of Newark, Mo. Received $5.00
Thursday	September 25, 1884	SILAS W. MYER married FANNIE GLOVER. Both of Knox County, Mo. Received $5.00

Thursday	October 16, 1884	GEORGE W. TAYLOR of Henry County, married MARTHA E. SCOTT of Knox County. Mo. Received $5.00
Thursday	December 25, 1884	E. H. KENNEY married ANNIE McVEY. Both of Shelby County, Mo. Received $5.00
PAGE 42		
Thursday	April 2, 1885	BENJAMIN F. NULL of Lewis County, married MARY L. HAYDEN of Knox County, Mo. Received $5.00
Thursday	December 17, 1885	JAMES J. HALDERMAN married SALLIE B. McCRACKEN. Both of Lewis County, Mo. Received $10.00
Thursday	October 21, 1886	ALEXANDER B. ROBERTS married SARAH E. BRISCOE. Both of Knox County, Mo. Received $5.00
Tuesday	November 30, 1886	HENRY S. BERRY married LYDA E. TULLY. Both of Knox County, Mo. Received $5.00
Thursday	March 10, 1887	CHARLES E. LEAR married LULA E. BERRY. Both of Knox County, Mo. Received $5.00
PAGE 43		
Thursday	September 29, 1887	GUY B. ROSS of Knox County, married MAGGIE L. STEWART of Lewis County, Mo. Received $5.00
Monday	January 30, 1888	GEORGE W. MYERS married INEY ABLETT. Both of Knox County, Mo. Received $4.00
Thursday	February 2, 1888	E. C STOKES married ELLA JOB. Both of Knox County, Mo. Received $4.00
Thursday	March 8, 1888	EARNEST J. PORTER of Lewis County, married SALLIE WITHERS of Knox County, Mo. Received $2.00
Sunday	July 1, 1888	ALBERT R. TODD married SUSIE S. BLAIR. Both of Knox County, Mo. Received $5.00

	PAGE 44	
Sunday	September 23, 1888	S. M. MYERS married THERESSA McEUTIRE. Both of Knox County, Mo. Received $5.00
Thursday	September 27, 1888	AMBROS MARTIN married SARAH A. HAYDON. Both of Knox County, Mo. Received $5.00
Tuesday	October 2, 1888	WILLIS E. ANDERSON of Plevira, Knox County, married Mrs. OLLIE K. THROCKMORTON of Newark, Mo. Received $10
Wednesday	February 13, 1889	W. A. GREEN of Ft. Smith, Arkansas married ADDUIE. HOHNES of Newark, Knox County, Mo. Received $10.00
Tuesday	December 24, 1889	JOHN T. COBBETT married ROBBIE L. OOWLES. Both of Knox County, Mo. Received $5.00
Wednesday	February 13, 1889	W. A. GREEN of Ft. Smith, Arkansas married ADDIE E. HOHNES of Newark, Knox County, Mo. Received $10.00
Tuesday	December 24, 1889	JOHN T. COBBETT married ROBBIE L. BEROLES. Both of Knox County, Mo. Received $5.00
	PAGE 45	
Monday	January 27, 1890	JEREMIOH MARTIN married NARCISSA J. SMITH. Both of Knox County, Mo. Received $7.00
Wednesday	February 26, 1890	S. P. McCRAKEN of Lewis County, married Mrs. LAURA A. DARE of Knox County, Mo. Received $8.00
Thursday	April 24, 1890	JOHN S. McREYNOLDS married ANNIE GLASSCOCK. Both of Knox County, Mo. Received $10.00
Thursday	December 24, 1891	JOSEPH F. WILLIS married LILLIAN L. ROSS. Both of Knox County, Mo. Received $5.00

Tuesday	January 31, 1893	JAMES B. RYLES of Montana, married NETTIE RUDEL of Knox County, Mo. Received $10.00
PAGE 46		
Tuesday	February 20, 1894	JOHN A. LANKFORD married LYDA M. PROSSER. Both of I, Knox County, Mo. Received $4.00
Thursday	October 11, 1894	RUBEN R. BOURN married CLARA R. LESLIR. Both of Knox County, Mo. Received $3.00
Thursday	November 1, 1894	JAMES B. SUTTON married CALLIE S. BERRY. Both of Knox County, Mo. Received $5.00
Thursday	June 29, 1895	CLIDE W. JONES of Lewis County, married JESSIE I. TRUE of Knox County, Mo. Received $5.00
PAGE 47		
Tuesday	October 31, 1899	WILLLIAM T. LaRUE of Lewis County, married Mrs. JENNIR BRENT F. BROWNING of Clark County, Mo. Received $12.00
Wednesday	January 10, 1900	DENNY L. KINNE married LULU R. PALMER. Both of Quincy, Illinois. (May have been Rev. Holt's granddaughter)

230 MARRIAGES

459 INDIVIDUALS

CHARLES MADISON HOLT

Born: August 28th, 1858, Dover, Lewis County, Missouri

Married: Elizabeth Marks, 1891, Quincy, Illinois

Died: January 30, 1931, Oklahoma City, Oklahoma

Interment: LaBelle Cemetery, Lot 27, Section 4, LaBelle, Missouri

Born the first son of the second marriage of James Madison Holt and Margaret Ann Mobley. His early childhood was spent in Dover, Lewis County, Liberty Clark County, and Newark Knox County. After attending local schools, he entered Missouri State University and graduated with a Law degree on March 27th, 1884. He returned to Knox City, Missouri and entered the practice of Law. His only bid for political office was for County Prosecutor in Knox County. He lost by two votes. He closed his law practice and moved to Quincy, Illinois.

On September 18th, 1890, he married Elizabeth Marks at the 1st Presbyterian Church of

La Grange, Missouri. From this union were born two sons: Harry Whitney Holt (1892-1980) and Paul Lawrence Holt (1894-1985) The young family made their home at 1006 York St., Quincy, Illinois.

The young attorney represented Otis Elevator Company of Chicago, Illinois, handling past due accounts and other legal matters. He was offered a position with the firm, which would require that he move to Chicago. In 1893, Charles took his wife, then carrying their second son, to Chicago to discuss the position, and visit the Worlds Fair. Walking about in a newly purchased pair of shoes, she became foot sore, and changed into an older pair of low cut shoes. This resulted in her catching a cold, which worsen when she returned to Quincy. She died of "consumption" shortly after giving birth to her second son, at the age of twenty-nine.

At this time, his father, mother and sister, Fannie E. Holt, moved to Quincy to care for his two sons and home. Charles continued to practice Law, but the loss of his young wife weighed heavily on him.

Sometime around 1900 (date unknown), Charles met and married Lottie Smoot in La Belle, Missouri. To this union was born a daughter, Julia Holt (Johnson) (1902-) Charles moved west with his new bride and older son, Harry. They resided in Helena, Montana for a short time and then settled in Denver, Colorado. He practiced Law and sold insurance in Denver. His office was located in the Ketterage Bank Building. Infidelity of Lottie brought about a divorce in 1904.

With the passing of his father in 1904, he returned to be with his mother, sister and his two sons. Julia remained with her mother in Denver. They made their home in La Belle. He became interested in a land venture with his brother-in-law, Luther Berry. Luther had sold his farm land in Missouri and purchased a larger farm in Cavour, South Dakota. Connected to the farm was a Feed Mill in Hurion.

Charles operated the Mill and Luther operated the farm. Cold weather and desire to return to Law practice and Insurance sales caused him to accept a position in Lawton, Oklahoma. He moved his Sister and two sons to Lawton about 1908. Both of his sons graduated high school from Lawton High School. In Lawton, Charles sold insurance for the Standard Accident Insurance Company, of Detroit, Michigan. In 1913 he was made the State Manager for this company and moved to Oklahoma City, Oklahoma. He purchased a home at 1619 Northwest 14th St. where he lived with his sister and two sons. He remained at this home during his retirement until his death in 1931

Luther Berry, Kate (Holt) Berry, Fannie Holt, and Charles Holt Picture taken about 1928.

59

HARRY WHITNEY HOLT

Born:	January 4, 1892, Quincy, Illinois
Married:	Millie in Oklahoma City, Evamae Casselberry in Dallas, Nell in Dallas (four times), and Kitty in Dallas (longest marriage)
Died:	June 6, 1980, 6111 Hudson Ave., Dallas, Texas
Interment:	La Belle Cemetery, Lot 27, Section 7. La Belle, Missouri

Born the first son of Charles Madison Holt and Elizabeth (Marks) Holt. He was just two years and six months old when his mother passed away. His aunt, Fannie E. Holt became his segregate mother. Shortly after the passing of his mother, he was taken by his Father, and Aunt to live with his Grandparents in La Belle, Missouri. His early education was begun in La Belle. Around 1900, his father remarried and he was taken to Denver, Colorado, where his Father practice Law and sold Insurance. His Father divorced Lottie, and the death of his Grandfather in 1904, caused his Father to move back to La Belle and reunite with his sister, his younger son and his Grand-Mother. He continued his elementary schooling in La Belle. Around 1905, his Uncle, Luther Berry

61

Harry's High School Graduation photo.

asked Charles, his Father to run a Feed Mill in Huron, South Dakota, which he had just purchased. This caused the family to move to Cavour, South Dakota. Harry was enrolled in school in Huron. The weather and his father's desire to return to the practice of Law, caused the family to move to Lawton, Oklahoma in 1908. Harry graduated from Lawton High School in 1911.

After graduating, he entered Oklahoma State College of Agriculture at Stillwater, Oklahoma. This later became University of Oklahoma. He completed his first year and began his living as a salesman. His first job was with the Dunnon Coconut Company of Oklahoma City. He traveled throughout Oklahoma as a salesman for this firm. The company expanded and he was given the

Harry Holt, forth from left, as a member of Lawton High School Basketball team, when he was a Senior at Lawton High School.

assignment of selling cigarettes by the pack. He suggested that they be packaged with ten packs in a carton, which would make them easier to handle and more profitable for the salesman. This idea was transferred to the manufacture and became standard for the industry.

During this period, he married his first wife, Milley, in Oklahoma City. He became attracted to the auto industry and joined

the Studebaker Corporation in Oklahoma City, contacting dealers. His desire to travel caused him to join Bastian-Morley Plumbing Supply of La Port, Indiana. He was assigned the State of Texas, located at Dallas, Texas. He traveled throughout Texas, contacting plumbing business, selling hot-water heaters, bathroom fixtures and assorted supplies. Since his initials were H.W. he soon became known as "Hot Water Holt."

The flexibility of being a salesman permitted him to enjoy his passion for hunting and fishing. He maintained a 32' Crisis-Craft on White Rock Lake outside Dallas, and often entertained the executives from Chicago on fishing and hunting trips.

It was in the late twenties that he married his second wife, Evamae Casselberry in Dallas, Texas. This ended in divorce. He then married Nell, who he married and divorced four times. In the late 1930s, he purchased a small farm near Plano, Texas. Around 1937, he married his last wife, "Kitty". She had a daughter from a previous marriage by

Harry in 1935 with a record fish he caught from the Gulf of Mexico.

Harry's Crisis-Craft speedboat on White Rock Lake outside of Dallas, Texas.

Harry's last wife, Kitty.

Harry with his adopted daughter, Gathernell.

the name of Gathernell. Harry adopted this daughter and she became the only child he considered his own.

Gathernell married Larry Henning and they had three children. She died very young and her children grew up never knowing their adopted Grandfather.

His marriage to Kitty lasted until 1946, ending when Kitty died in an auto accident in 1957. Harry sold his farm in 1946 and purchased the Allis Chalmers Implement Dealership in Kaufman, Texas. He operated that business until 1958. He retired at the age of sixty-four and continued to live at his residence, at 6111 Hudson, Dallas, Texas.

In September of 1958, his nephew, Paul L. Holt Jr., was appointed the American Motors dealer in Hamilton, Ohio. Since Holt Implement had not been sold, Harry offered his shop equipment to his nephew, and took a note for the balance, which was paid with interest shortly thereafter.

On March 19, 1978, his nephew made a trip to Dallas with a 1970 Lincoln Town Car, which he had taken in trade and had reconditioned to perfection. He presented Harry with this car to replace an older Ford that needed much repair. Knowing how much his Uncle liked big luxury cars, Harry was pleased. At this visit, his nephew made a recording of Harry's life, much of which is in this biography.

Harry, left, and his brother, Paul Holt, Sr.

The picture above left was taken after his nephew, Paul Holt, presented Harry with a new car in 1978. At the right is the last picture taken of Harry W. Holt. He died in the heat wave of June 6, 1980. He was one of six people who expired that day. The air conditioner in his front bedroom malfunctioned and this caused his death.

PAUL LAWRENCE HOLT SR.

Born: June 17, 1894, Quincy, Illinois

Married: Louise Edmonia Welsh, August 18, 1925, Oklahoma City

Died: February 9, 1985, New Carlisle, Ohio

Interment: Lot 185, Block 7, Fairlawn Cemetery, Oklahoma City, Okla.

Born the second son of Charles Madison Holt and Elizabeth (Marks) Holt. His mother passed away shortly after his birth. Fannie E. Holt, his aunt, became the only maternal parent he knew. Later his father, aunt, and older brother moved to La Belle, Missouri, where his Grandfather Holt served as the local Baptist Minister. He recalled his first job after school, as a juvenile, was cleaning out and restocking the local hardware store in La Belle, after school.

Shortly after the death of his Grandfather in 1904, his father, aunt, and older brother moved to Cavour, South Dakota. Luther Berry, Charles Holt's brother-in-law, operated a feed mill and general store in that community. Paul L Holt attended elementary school in Huron, South Dakota. In 1908, his father, aunt, older brother Harry and fourteen-year old Paul moved to Lawton,

Paul at 17 years old in Lawton, Okla., April 1912.

Paul in 1920.

Oklahoma, where his father resumed his law practice and entered the insurance business. Both his older brother Harry, and Paul graduated from Lawton High School. The picture at the left is his high school graduation picture. After graduating in 1912, he worked at a local bookstore for $6 a week. He attended business school in the evenings, learning typing and bookkeeping.

As a youth, Holt always enjoyed playing baseball, mainly as a shortstop between second and third base. Several years later, because of his skillful ability, he was asked to try out for a professional farm team; but his father believed that Paul would be better off to join Ford Motor Company. Holt was a lifelong fan of baseball and the Chicago Cubs.

His father's insurance business prospered and he was offered the position of State Manager of Standard Accident Insurance of Detroit. This required the family to move to Oklahoma City, Oklahoma, around 1913. Young Paul was employed by an attorney, doing bookwork and clerking for various local businesses.

On September 15, 1915, Paul L. Holt joined Ford Motor Company Branch at Oklahoma City. Beginning in the Parts Department, he proceeded to move to more important assignments in accounting, as a teller, and finally into the sales department. It was during these years that he made friends with a fellow worker, Felix Dorand, and both men came under the watchful eye of H.C. Doss, the current Branch Manager.

on March 15th, 1918. He was made Sergeant 1/C1 on June 8, 1918.

His squadron opened the newly formed AVIATION GENERAL SUPPLY DEPOT, commonly described as AGSD. He witnessed the fatal crash of Lt. Patterson, who was killed firing a machine gun through the propeller of his aircraft. The crash occurred close to the building where AGSD was located. This base is now named Wright-Patterson Air Force Base.

Holt related to his family that some time in 1918, he contracted the flu during the 1918 pandemic flu, which was estimated to have caused over 500,000 deaths in the U.S. He was hospitalized and told by the man in the bed next to him that he was in the "death" ward, and no one left the ward alive. Holt

St. 1st Class Paul Lawrence Holt at the time of enlistment in the Aviation Signal Corps in 1918.

On December 12, 1917, Paul Holt enlisted in the Aviation Section of the Army Signal Corp. at Fort Logan, Colorado. He was assigned to the 678th Aero Squadron and sent to Kelly Field, South San Antonio, Texas. He was advanced to Sergeant of the 678th Aero Squadron at Osborn (now Fairfield) Ohio

Paul with his fellow servicemen when he was assigned to the 628 Aero Squadron at Garden City, Long Island, N.Y. on October 4,1918.

made up his mind that he would regain his health and walk out alive.

Prior to his transfer to the 628th he was assigned as an Aviation Cadet to U.S.S.M.A. Princeton Ground School, Princeton, N.J. In the final stages of WW1, the 628th Squadron processed incoming personnel from Europe. He was Honorably Discharged on February 20, 1919.

Returning to Oklahoma City in March of 1919, he was re-employed by Ford Motor Co. He was transferred from the Parts Department to the Branch Office as Purchasing Agent, then transferred to the Sales Department as a Territory Manager (Roadman). He progressed to Car Distribution, Wholesale Manager and was finally Sales Manager of the Oklahoma City Branch.

In 1924, he was directed to place an ad in the local Oklahoma City newspaper. The young girl who took the ad was Louise Welsh, who was working a summer job between semesters at the University of Oklahoma. Holt was attracted to her and asked the Office Manager, whom he knew, to introduce him as "he would put a ring on her finger." This began a courtship that resulted in their marriage on August 18, 1925.

The wedding party: Earleen Welsh and Stacy Welsh, mother and father of the bride, Louise Welsh, bride, Paul Holt Sr. groom, Fannie E. Holt, aunt of the groom, Charles Holt, father of the groom. From this marriage, two children were born: Paul Lawrence Holt Jr. on May 29, 1926 and Barbara Louise Holt on August 12, 1935.

Paul in 1925.

They were married at the Presbyterian Church on 28th Street, Oklahoma City, OK. Fairlawn Cemetery is in the rear of the church, where they both are interned.

In 1925, Holt was appointed Assistant Branch Manager of the newly formed Des Moines, Iowa Branch of Ford Motor Company. In 1927 the Branch Manager resigned, and he was appointed Acting Branch Manager. At the beginning of 1930, there were 34 Ford Branches in the United States. Henry

Ford was shocked by the rapid fall in sales and the decline on Wall Street after the October 1929 "crash", so he instructed Harry Bennet to cut expenses at all Branches.

His team visited the Branches with three main goals: First, cancel all local civic support; Second, eliminate all Advertising expense; and Third, terminate any employee who was making more than $600 per month. All Branch Managers and Assistant Managers, with the exception of two, were terminated. The two survivors took smaller salaries and remained with Ford Motor Company.

This was the greatest blunder Henry Ford made as he had terminated his most experienced and talented executives. General Motors hired many of these men and the market share for Chevrolet increased, even in a declining market. Chevrolet took first place in domestic sales and didn't relinquish it until 2007.

Holt found himself separated from Ford in January 1930. He later received a personal letter from Henry Ford asking him to return to the company; however, the bitterness of his termination prevented him from accepting the offer. He spent most of 1930 traveling with his wife and son throughout Canada and the United States. In the fall of 1930, his old friend, Felix

Charles M. Holt and Paul L. Holt Sr. holding a young Paul L Holt Jr in 1929.

Doran, now a Regional Manager with Chevrolet, contacted him and offered to arrange an interview with the home office of Chevrolet in Detroit. He was hired by Chevrolet and assigned to the Oklahoma City Zone, where he organized a five-day salesman/dealer school. Detroit approved this program and adopted it throughout the nation.

He was next sent to Fort Worth, Texas, where he trained new road representatives. He next was assigned as District Manager to Altus, Oklahoma, then to Tulsa, Oklahoma,

and then to Lubbock, Texas, in the spring of 1935. He was assigned to Des Moines Zone. He served several positions in the Des Moines Zone and worked with Paul Manning, car distributor at that time. In the spring of 1937 he was transferred to Janesville, Wisconsin Chevrolet Zone. He served several positions in that zone.

It had been the practice of the Chevrolet Zone to hold a Departmental meeting every Monday morning. The meeting of December 8, 1941, was a somber one. Most of the discussion was about the attack on Pearl Harbor and how it would affect each of their lives. When the Zone Manager, Mr. Harrison, arrived, he read a telegram that he had just received from Detroit. He was instructed to retain his secretary and remain in his office. All other personnel were to be advised that their employment would end on December 15th. Vacation pay would be added to their final pay. They were to have finished all their contacts and clean out their personal effects by that date.

Roadmen were to either purchase their assigned cars or turn them in on that date. Employment would be guaranteed after the war, if personnel wished to return to General Motors. Production of cars was to continue until parts were exhausted. No shipments of cars were to be made, as all cars were impounded for possible government use.

Holt purchased his road car, a 1942 Chevrolet Deluxe two-door sedan. He was concerned that the government might impound the second car of anyone with two cars in a family, so he sold Louise's 1941 Chevrolet Deluxe four-door sedan.

The Zone Manager called Holt into his office the following day and explained that he was needed to work on an Army Mobile Communication vehicle mounted on a Chevrolet chassis, which was being assembled in Chicago. He would be working as a civilian and reporting to the Army.

He left the following week and filled that position for the next five months. Holt applied for a commission and was given the rank of Captain in the Air Force (Serial # 0 485343). He was sent to Miami, Florida, for Officer training on July 24, 1942. After training, he was ordered to report to Spokane Depot, Spokane, Washington, for further transfer. After reporting, he went to the Officer's mess hall for dinner, and was surprised to meet a former employee of Ford Motor Company who he had worked with in Des Moines, Iowa.

He was invited to have dinner with this officer and his superior officer. Throughout dinner, this

Louise Welsh Holt, about 1940.

Paul at his desk in 1943.

Colonel kept asking Holt about his work with General Motors and Ford. At the conclusion of the dinner, the Colonel turned to Holt and stated that he would have his orders changed the next morning and he would be assigned to the Fourth Echelon Repair Unit of the Maintenance Division, as the Colonel's Assistant. This division organized the repair and maintenance of B-17s and B-24 heavy bombers returning from Europe.

While working at the Chevrolet Zone Office at Oklahoma City, Holt met William S. Knudsen. Both men had worked for Ford Motor Company, and had many friends with the old company. Knudsen was the architect for Ford Motor Branches built in the early 1920s. His patterns were carried forward and included the new Branch at Des Moines, built in 1924.

William S. Knudsen had been born and educated in Copenhagen and came to America as an adult. His first job in the U.S. was with the Seabury Shipyards at Morris Heights, New Jersey. He then went to the Gas Engine and Power Company at Morris Heights, New Jersey. His next job was with John Keirn Mills at Buffalo, New York. He handled an order from Oldsmobile for 4,000 brake drums in 1905.

Ford Motors acquired Keim Mills in 1911, and that's how Knudsen began his work with Ford Motor Company. Knudsen set up 27 assembly plants in Branches throughout America for Ford. Around 1920, Knudsen began to have disagreements with Henry Ford, resulting in his departure from the company.

C.S. Mott enticed Knudsen to join G.M. and when Alfred Sloan was seeking a new manager for Chevrolet in 1921, Mott suggested that Knudsen was the man for that job. William S. Knudsen became General Manager of Chevrolet Division in 1932. He guided that Division to its first record production of 208,848 units. He continued to guide that Division, making inroads on Ford, the largest domestic producer in the U.S.

In February 1931, Holt was hired by Chevrolet Division in Detroit and assigned to the Oklahoma Zone Office. Since they had both worked at Ford, they shared many acquaintances, including Felix Doran, who had been Holt's best man at his wedding.

Knudsen was made Executive Vice-President of General Motors on October 15, 1933. In 1937, Knudsen was named President of General Motors. He served until June 1940, when he resigned to serve on the Advisory Commission to the Council on National Defense.

At the outbreak of war, Knudsen was commissioned a Lieutenant General and placed in charge of mobilizing manufacturing to supply the war effort. With this background, an interesting event took place at Spokane Air Depot mid-year 1943.

All Officers of Spokane Air Depot were invited to attend a luncheon at the Officers Club. They were invited to hear a speech by Lt. General Knudsen. Knudsen and the Base Commander greeted everyone. When Holt's turn arrived, Knudsen recognized him and gave him a warm greeting. The two visited for several minutes, until the Base Commander suggested the line was being held up and they needed to greet all the officers before the luncheon could begin. Knudsen agreed and parted with Holt saying, "See me after the meeting."

The purpose of this meeting was to present Spokane Air Depot with the "E" flag, given to only those suppliers and companies who attained Excellence by meeting their quotas in the war effort. The following week, the Base Commander ordered Holt to his office. He explained that he needed an officer who could handle a difficult assignment.

After the discussion with Gen. Knudsen, Holt was to be given this assignment. He was not to tell anyone, including his family, what he would be doing. Secrecy was most important. Holt would maintain his office at Spokane Air Depot reporting only to the Base Commander. He was assigned to secure construction workers for several projects needed by the Base and also an important project

Paul in 1944.

on the Columbia River, which needed to be called a "power plant."

He was to travel throughout Washington State and Northern Oregon to recruit personnel to work on these projects. All recruits would receive draft deferments and wages according to their ability, and would be processed at Spokane Air Depot. Since most construction workers had been taken by the draft, they needed people who could do construction on large projects.

Holt was told that the "Power Plant" on the Columbia River was more than just a power plant. It was part of the Manhattan Project, and important to the war effort. As Holt was leaving, the Commander said, "Holt you're being promoted to Major. I've Processed the paperwork and it will be effective the first of the month. Congratulations!"

When that assignment was complete, Holt was assigned to close the auxiliary Air Base at Cut Bank, Montana, in 1945. He was honorably discharged as a Major in July 1945.

Desiring to settle down, he returned to Janesville, Wisconsin, and purchased a home at 1027 Ruger Ave. He declined the offer to rejoin Chevrolet Motor Division and began to pursue the Firestone franchise for Janesville. Unable to reach an agreement with the current owner, he settled on a Coast-to-Coast Hardware franchise.

His store was located on North Milwaukee Street in the spring of 1946. After the war, almost every retail operation was short of items that were not available during the war. Washing machines, lawn mowers, refrigerators, stoves, garden tools, almost any item a homeowner needed were all in short supply.

Coast-to-Coast headquarters in Minneapolis promised Holt a fair share of these items, but never delivered. The home office took care of their old-line dealers first and newer dealers suffered the shortages. Holt sold the store back to the central office in the summer of 1948.

With his background in the automobile field, Holt set out to find an automobile franchise in or near Janesville. The Ford franchise in Delavan, Wisconsin, was available, so Holt and his son made a trip to Chicago to talk to the Regional Manager.

Mr. Edmonds was an old friend of Holt's — they'd worked together at Ford. The planning potential at Delavan was three cars a month, but Ford wanted a new building, which would have cost $150,000. To service this investment, Holt reasoned that a reasonable allotment needed would be ten units a month. As much as Edmonds wanted to accommodate him, he was being controlled by Detroit and was unable to increase the allotment.

After the meeting, Holt and his son checked into the Drake Hotel. The banner at the registration desk read: "WELCOME NASH DEALERS". Holt thought he remembered reading that his old mentor, H.C. Doss, had been made General Sales Manager of Nash.

Checking at the desk, he called Mr. Doss and was invited to his suite. Both Holt and his son were invited to the 1949 Nash Announcement meeting the next day at the hotel. Holt was impressed with the newly designed "Airflow" Nash. After talking with several dealers, whom he knew, he was convinced that a Nash franchise was an opportunity he should pursue. H.C. Doss introduced him to three Zone Managers, and before the day was out, he had been offered four dealer points to consider. Mr. Doss's last comment to Holt was, "We want you as a Nash dealer."

After reviewing the dealer points offered, Holt and his son made a trip to Columbus, IN. This was a small city of twelve thousand, forty miles south of Indianapolis. It was the home of Cummins Diesel Engine, Arvin Industries, and Cosco Kitchen Ware. With the industries, a downtown location (3rd & Franklin), and the current owner wanted out — this the opportunity Holt wanted. He completed the purchase and opened Holt Nash on October 10, 1948.

Holt and his son operated the agency successfully, and made plans to make their home in Columbus as soon as Holt's daughter, Bobbie Lou Holt, finished her school year in 1949. However, Louise Holt did not want to leave her home (**pictured on right**) and her friends in Janesville.

She made several trips to Columbus, but was not convinced to move. Holt's son returned to the University of Wisconsin in the fall of 1950, and Holt sold his dealership to Mr. John Thompson of Muncie, IN in the spring of 1951.

Returning to Janesville, he was approached by the Wyoming Valley Equipment Company of Wilkes-Barre, PA. This company sold

Paul and Louise at their 50th wedding anniversary on August 18, 1975.

specialized digging attachments, which were mounted on medium-duty Chevrolet and Ford trucks. Mainly public utility companies used these attachments.

As Regional Sales Manager, he was back on the road traveling mostly in the midwestern states. He later joined Texacoma Equip-

The Holt home in Janesville, Wisc. The Holts lived here from 1945 through 1979.

ment Company and served this company until his retirement in 1973.

Paul L. Holt Sr. was never elected to public office, but was a lifetime registered Republican. He was a member of the Masonic Fraternity and held the 32nd degree in the Oklahoma City Lodge. He was a past member of the Janesville Rotary Club. He was appointed to the Janesville Library Board in 1974 and served until 1979.

Both he and his wife, Louise, considered Janesville their permanent residence. They lived at 1524 Ruger Ave. from 1937 until 1942, and at 1027 Ruger Ave. from 1945 until 1979. Their last residence was 403 Villa Dr., New Carlisle, Ohio.

Holt passed away on Feb. 9, 1985. Louise remained on Villa Dr. until 1992 and then moved to Brookhaven Retirement Home. She passed away on August 18, 1999, which would have been Paul and Louise's 74th wedding anniversary.

PAUL LAWRENCE HOLT JR.

Born: May 29, 1926, Des Moines, Iowa

Married: Louise Miller, March 25, 1956, Eaton, Ohio

Died:

Interment: Interment: West Ghester Municipal Cemetery, Lot 76A

The only son of Paul L. and Louise (Welsh) Holt. His father traveled for both Ford Motor Company and General Motors, and the family moved often. He attended grammar school in Des Moines, Iowa; Fort Worth, Texas; Altus, Oklahoma; Tulsa, Oklahoma; Lubbock, Texas; Des Moines, Iowa (second time); and Janesville, Wisconsin. He started high school in Janesville.

In the middle of his Junior year, the family moved to Spokane, Washington, where his father was stationed at Spokane Air Depot He graduated from Lewis & Clark High School on June 6, 1944. All high school graduates were being drafted into military service after their eighteenth birthday, unless they enlisted in a branch of service of their choice. Holt selected the U.S. Navy, and enlisted May 15, 1944.

He was called into service on August 11, 1944 and sent to Great Lakes, Illinois for Boot Camp. He served the Navy until August 18,1946, and was honorably discharged at

CLASS LEADERS New officers of the 100th 12A Lewis and Clark high school graduating class are, left to right: Stan Kaufman, secretary; Paul Holt, treasurer; Jack Krehibel, vice president, and Vivian Ahlstedt, president. Patty Dugger, not present when the picture was taken, is fifth executive.

Boston, Massachusetts. He returned to Janesville, Wisconsin and entered the University of Wisconsin, Madison in the fall of 1946.

In February 1948, he left the University to assist his father in their Coast-to-Coast Hardware store. He re-entered the University in the fall of 1950, and continued until August 1952. He majored in Finance and Marketing.

When he left the University, he lacked six credits for his BBA degree, but had completed all required courses for his degree. In the fall of 1952, while working for Buick Motor Division, he took a night course in physiology at the University of Dayton, gaining three credits. In 1992, after selling his business, he took two courses in Computer Science, at Sinclair College, Dayton, thus completing his requirements for his BBA degree on May 16th, 1993. He is listed as a graduate in 1993, however he is more associated with the class of 1952.

While attending the 7th grade, his mother began giving him piano lessons. Piano did not appeal to him, so his father purchased a cornet for him, which seemed to be more to his liking. As his entered Junior High School, he took lessons from Mr. Herman Helbig, the High School Band Director. He was a member of the Janesville High School Band in 8th, 9th, 10th, and 11th grade.

In the middle of his junior year of High School, his family moved to Spokane, Washington, where he was a member of Lewis & Clark High School Band. He played second trumpet to Wally Burdge. Wally was the lead trumpet in a dance band led by Johnny Powell. Wally asked Holt to join him in the dance band and Holt accepted. He purchased a new trumpet to match the gold instruments others had in the band.

Their first engagement was a dance at the Spokane Country Club. There were eleven members in the band, Johnny Powell, drummer, Brad Young, piano, Joe Long saxophone. I remember we were paid $10 for about two hours of dinner music. This was great — he was now a paid professional.

Soon, this band was playing every Friday night at the Desert Hotel, and several nights at the Natatorium Park in Spokane. We played for two Prom dances at the University of Washington, Pullman, Washington. We were mentioned in an article in *Life* maga-

zine. When most of the members graduated from high school, they entered military service, and the band disbanded.

Holt again became active in music in December of 1945. Stationed at Brunswick, Maine, the Navy Band attached to the Air Base, was transferred. This left the Base without music for the weekly Friday night enlisted men dance and the twice-monthly Officers dance. Several Enlisted men and Officers gathered together and with a few students from Bowdoin College formed a dance band to supply music for these dances. Holt traveled to Portland, Maine and ordered orchestrations and band stands for this new band. Soon they were playing every Wednesday night for the U.S.O. Dance in Brunswick, as well as the Base dances. Twice, they were

invited to play for Prom dances at Bowdoin College.

When the band played on the base, we used twelve members. When we played at the USO and outside engagements, we used only eight members. The last dance played at the Brunswick Naval Air Station was July 4, 1946. Bob Madden purchased the orchestrations and the band stands from Holt and formed his own group while attending the University of Maine at Augusta, ME. Later, Madden became a Senator in the Maine State Senate.

In the summers of 1937-1939, Holt was a member of the local YMCA and spent most of his summer at the Y. He enjoyed swimming, playing table tennis and other activities. In the summer of 1939, the YMCA

Pictured at are Ens. Irv Nelson on saxophone (from California), Lt. Hume on drums (he was later killed on takeoff at Norfolk, Va.), Bob Madden on trombone, a student from Bowdoin on clarinet, Holt on trumpet, bass player stationed at Brunswick, Ens., and Don Gillis from Kansas City, Mo. on piano.

offered a program of Marksmanship. Rifles and ammunition were supplied by the Government and the National Guard Armory was used as the rifle range. The Government was preparing for the future conflict.

The National Rifle Association awarded medals for the achievement of various stages of advancement. Holt progress from Pro-Marksman, Marksman, and the eight levels of Sharpshooter while in Janesville. Expert and finally Distinguished Rifleman levels were earned while a member of the Lewis & Clark High School Rifle Team in Spokane, Washington. His first competitive rifle match was the Junior State Championship held in Racine, Wisconsin on May 31, 1941. He placed first in Class B, winning his first medal.

Five members of the A team won the three position National Intercollegiate Rifle Match held at Chicago, with a score of 1341, with the University of Cincinnati scoring 1338, the University of Minnesota scoring 1332, and Ohio State scoring 1322. This was the first time University of Wisconsin had won the Big Ten College Match.

Holt placed second on the A Team, giving him a medal. Holt held the university record for a four position score of 394 until his teammate, John Thompson, broke it with a score of 396. I understand that record still stands. Holt's last competitive rifle match was the Indiana State Rifle Association, Wabash Valley Rifle League Match, held at Terre Haute, Indiana in the summer of 1950. He won three trophies and two medals.

The Janesville Junior Rifle Team of 1940.

The University of Wisconsin Rifle Team of 1947. Shown are: Major Burns, Coach, first row left; John Thompson (teammate) first row, second from left; Paul Holt, first row, third from right; Robert Bohm, Captain of the Team, first row, second from right. Sorry that the names of other members of the team are not available.

After graduation from Lewis & Clark High School in Spokane on June 6, 1944, he enlisted into the U.S. Navy. He was called up on August 18th and sent to Great Lakes, Illinois for Boot Camp. The training was intense, but his physical condition improved and was the best it had ever been.

After Boot Camp, he was given leave to return to Spokane. Then went to Chicago, where he was assigned to Hugh Manley High School for additional training. There, he was reunited with Richard C. Yancey, a fellow classmate from Lewis & Clark High School.

Holt had some knowledge of Chicago, since his parents had taken him there many times. He was pleased to show Dick around the "Loop." It was Christmastime and the shops and streets were packed. While walking past some of the display windows, a voice shouted out, "Paul Holt!" and two young girls, Charlotte and Marilyn McCue, came rushing up to meet the young sailors. The McCue sisters had been classmates of Holt at Janesville High School. Holt introduced Yancey to his former classmates and invited the sisters to accompany them to a movie. They accepted.

After the movie, the girls were treated to a soda at a local ice cream shop. Holt and Yancey escorted the girls to local "Elevator" station where they caught the next train to their home in Oak Park. The girls invited Holt and Yancey to lunch the following day at their home, in Oak Park. Holt and Yancey accepted and spent the following afternoon at the McCue's home in Oak Park. It was so unusual that the girls would find an old classmate while walking down a jam-packed street of Christmas shoppers, on Chicago's busiest thoroughfare.

While at Hugh Manley High School, Holt mentioned he had been trained as a Qualified Link Trainer Instructor. He had earned this status while working a summer job at Spokane Air Depot in 1943. This information was related to his superiors, and Holt was transferred to Navy Pier for further transfer. In December of 1944, Holt was sent to Oglethorpe Naval Air Station, Georgia, along with twelve ex-Air Cadets. They were to be trained as Naval link Trainer Operators.

While most of the Navy Link Instructors were WAVES (females), not all Air Stations had facilities for WAVES, so it was necessary to have male operators.

Our class of thirteen were the only males in the school of over four hundred WAVES students. The ex-Air Cadets were all in their early twenties, except Holt, who was eighteen. Since the WAVES students were restricted to their barracks at nine o'clock, our class did not come in contact with them. However, the female instructors had liberty whenever they wanted. Two of our classmates ended up married to instructors.

After completing training at Oglethorpe, Holt and five of his classmates were sent to Quonset Point, Rhode Island for further training in Celestial Navigation. These Link Trainers were not mobile and required a building built around the trainers. After three weeks, Holt, Brown and Ketchum were assigned to Lewis-Auburn Air Station, about thirty miles north of Portland, Maine.

They arrived on May 5, 1945, after a five-inch snowstorm that downed the electrical power to the Air Station. Lewis-Auburn was a small community that was supported by three or four large woolen mills. The naval officers were housed off base at local hotels. This Air Station served as a training base for TBM Squadrons, which were reformed from new pilots and those returning from combat in the Pacific.

Because Naval Pilots flew over water with no visual reference available, it was necessary that they be proficient in radio navigation. Each pilot was required to have six hours per year in radio navigation in order to keep his pilot status. These lessons were given in thirty-minute segments, as pilots detested these lessons.

Our training Department consisted of Stan Shaut, a former pilot, Brown, Ketchum and Holt. We had two officers who were in charge, but we seldom saw them. The four operators were kept busy with training, since the TBM squadrons were rotated often. All operators were "ship company" and quartered in the second floor of Barracks #1, along with the Marine Guard. We sometimes were call on to man the telephone watch at the headquarters.

On August 15, 1945, the war in the Pacific ended, and the celebration began. It seemed that everyone in the area converged on Lewis-Auburn, as the city streets were overflowing with citizens and sailors. Most officers took off for Portland, Boston and New York. Holt was on liberty at a movie when the house lights came on and the manager announced that the War was over.

I thought it ironic that the two biggest drunks in Ship Company had been made S.P.

(Shore Patrol). Holt caught a bus back to the base a little after midnight. There were no guards at the entrance and the base was all but deserted. The next morning, everyone fixed their own breakfasts, as there were no cooks available. Shortly after this, Ketchum, Shaut, Brown and Holt were transferred to Brunswick Naval Air Station, Brunswick, Maine.

Discharges from the service were arranged on a point system, with each month counting. Points also were given for months in combat zones. Since Holt had a shorter service and no combat service, he was discharged on July 18, 1946 at Boston, Massachusetts.

Holt returned to where his parents had moved in Janesville, Wisconsin. His father had opened a Hardware Store in the middle of Janesville. Holt found himself clerking on the afternoon of July 20th. He began school at the University of Wisconsin, Madison, in the fall semester of 1946. University enrollment had exploded with all the servicemen returning and taking advantage of the G.I. Bill.

Ohio State was the largest of the big ten schools, with over 23,000 enrolled. Wisconsin enrollment was over 18,000 students. Quonsets Huts were erected for classrooms and local churches were used for lecture halls.

Taken shortly after Lewis-Auburn Air Station was closed. Front row left, unknown, Bill Brown, Joe Cox, Helen Fox. Back row left Bill & Mary Kohn, Betsy Ross, Ketchum, Hazel (Farris) Schoonover, Jane Ross. Middle row center unknown, Elkland, and Stan Shaut.

The Brunswick Training Dept. in the spring of 1946. Front row left unknown, unknown, Holt, unknown, Lucien Valance. Back row left Hazel (Ferris) Schoonover, Helen Fox, unknown, Lt. Com. Duncan Van Norden, unknown (she married Lucien), and unknown. Sorry that names are not available for so many.

Lines formed, sometimes for three blocks, to register for classes or buy books.

Housing was also difficult for students. Holt shared a room in a private residence with another student for his first semester. He was able to enter Bodkin Hall on campus for the spring semester. Because of the large enrollment, the university offered a full semester in the summer of 1946. Holt registered for the full semester to help with his desire to catch up with his classmates.

After four full semesters in a row, he was worn-out, so he returned to Janesville to help his father with the hardware store. When Holt's father was offered a chance to sell his store to an employee of the franchisee, he agreed. Thus, in April 1948, Holt and his father began looking for an Auto Agency.

Holt's father had many friends in the Des Moines, Iowa area, so the two went to Des Moines. While visiting an old friend, Paul Manning of Paul Manning Chevrolet Inc., Mr. Manning suggested that young Holt come to work for his agency and learn "the trade."

The following week, young Holt began his training as a Service Writer, then as Parts Counter Man, and finally as a Floor Greeter. Since new cars were still in high demand, his training as a salesman was not extensive. Lou Backrod was the Sales Manager at the time.

He later was able to take the Chevrolet Dealership in Rockford, Illinois.

Holt's father calls him late in July, stating he was working on the Ford Agency in Delevan, Wisconsin, and felt he should return to Janesville. This agency required a new building, which would cost around $150,000. The allotment for Delevan was three new cars a month. Holt's father knew that the operation would require at least ten cars a month to service the debt incurred for the new building, so he arranged a meeting with the Regional Manger of Ford in Chicago. Young Holt accompanied his father to Chicago to meet with Mr. Edmonds, the Regional Manager.

Since Holt Sr. and Edmonds had worked together when Holt had worked for Ford, the meeting was very cordial. Edmonds stated he would make the request to Detroit for a recommendation to increase the allotment, however he doubted it would be approved.

Holt and his father checked into the Drake Hotel that afternoon. As the entered the Drake, a large sign in the lobby over the registration desk stated "WELCOME NASH DEALERS". Holt Sr. turned to the clerk at the desk and asked if H. C. Doss was registered. The clerk replied yes, and gave them his suite number.

Holt Sr. then called to the suite and asked to speak to Mr. Doss. He and his son were invited to his suite. Mr. Doss had been Branch

Manager of Ford Motors in Oklahoma City when Holt Sr. started working for Ford in 1914. When Holt Sr. entered the room, it was like a family reunion, since the two had not seen each other for over twenty years.

When Doss found out Holt Sr. was looking for a dealership, he responded, "We want you as a Nash Dealer." Doss summoned four Zone Managers to meet with Holt Sr. and said, "Get this man a Dealership!" Before the Holts left the room, Holt Sr. was offered four dealer points to consider, and invited to the new car showing at the Hotel the next day.

The following day, Nash Dealers from the Central Region were shown the 1949 Airflyte Nash, which was a completely redesigned automobile. Holt Sr. began to reconsider Fords offer and promised he would look into what Nash was offering. After reviewing the points offered, he decided to make a trip to Columbus, Indiana.

Columbus, Indiana was a small town of about twelve thousand, forty miles south of Indianapolis. It had three main manufacturing facilities: Cummins Diesel (Motors), Arvin Industries (Mufflers) and CASCO (kitchenware). After talking with the previous owner, who had other interests, Holt's father struck a deal. A series of meetings followed, arranging for floor plan, establishing banking arrangements, and signing Nash

Above is the Holt Nash Company, at 3rd & Franklin in Columbus, Indiana. This photo was taken in the spring of 1949. Today, the building has been taken over by Cummins Motors and is used as their training center. It is located one block east of the County Courthouse.

agreements. Holt Nash began operating on Oct. 10, 1948.

Holt Nash operated from Oct. 1948 until April 1951. The business was then sold to John Thompson of Muncie, Indiana, who later became a Buick Dealer in Connersville, Indiana. Paul Holt Jr. remained working for his father until August of 1950, then returned to the family home in Janesville.

After that, he re-entered the University of Wisconsin, Madison to begin the fall semester.

Sam Soffa, taken while attending the University.

88

Holt was assigned a room at Bodkins Hall, University Dormitory. His roommate was Sam Soffa from Fond du Lac, Wisconsin. Sam's father had operated an Auto Repair Shop in Fond du Lac. The two had similar auto work experience and formed a friendship, which has lasted a lifetime.

Sam was asked by several of his Fond du Lac High School classmates to join their fraternity, Phi Sigma Kappa. Sam asked Holt if he would join with him. Holt agreed. Together, they moved into the old German House off Landon Street and joined the fraternity.

Sam made contact with a company that sold knives and kitchenware called Cutco. He received leads from the company's advertising, and then set up personal house calls. This arrangement let him study and attend classes during the day, while making his sales presentations during the evening. At one time, he became the leading salesman for the central region of Wisconsin.

Holt found the local Nash agency to be just off campus, so he applied for a part-time position. Harvey Ray, was part owner of Nash Madison, having been the sales-man-

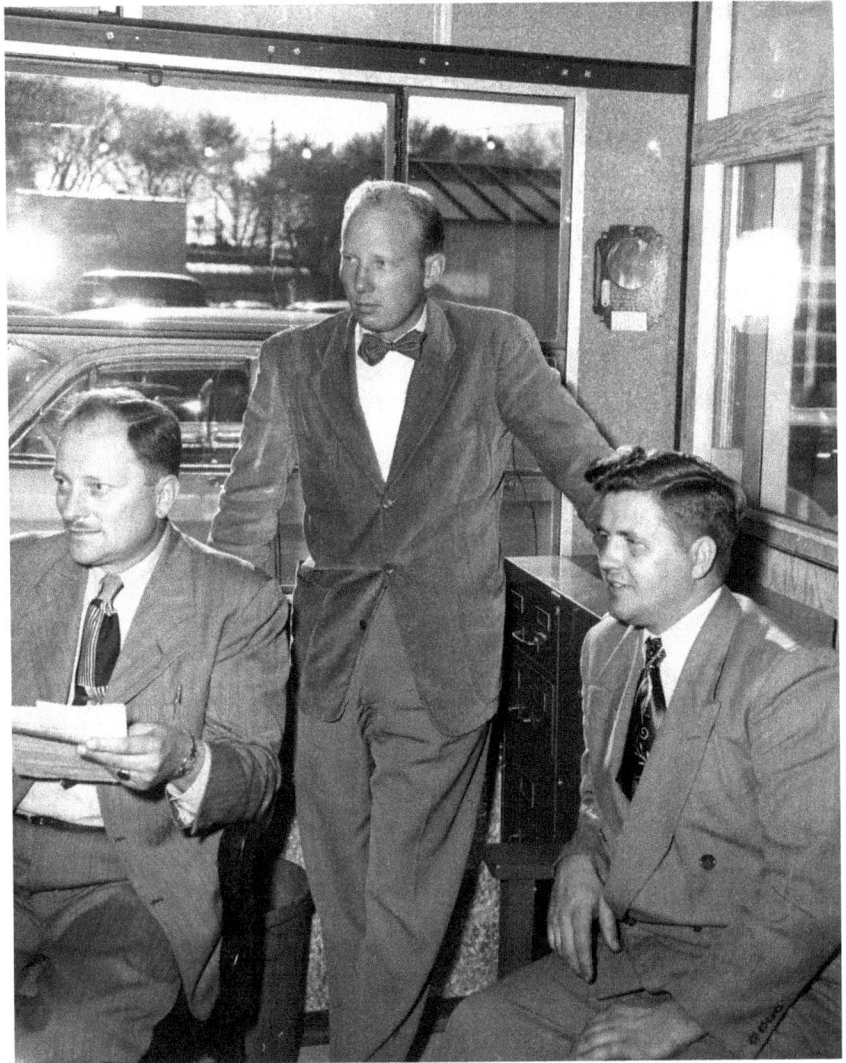

Harry Christenson, Paul Holt and Howard Kopon, who was a buyer for Christenson, in 1951 at 1136 East Washington Street.

ager of the Buick Dealership in Terre Haute, Indiana. The other owner was a local Attorney. Holt was hired to organize their Parts Department. When that was finished, he was given the job of setting up a Sales Training program for newly hired salesmen, who had never sold cars. He was also used in the Sales Department, whenever the sales staff attended meetings. In the spring of 1951, the Used Car Manager of Nash Madison, Mr. Harry Christenson,

Resigned to form his own Used Car Lot on Auto Row, East Washington Ave., north of the State Capitol, Christenson asked Holt to join him. Since Holt had arranged his classes in the morning, he would be able to spend afternoons at the lot. This arrangement was good for both Holt and Christenson. This freed Christenson to look for inventory and run errands, and permitted Holt to supplement his college expenses and still pursue his college degree.

Holt took summer courses in 1951 and 1952, which enabled him to complete all requirements for his Bachelor degree. With only six elective credits left, he determined it was time to secure permanent employment, and began his search in Chicago.

The Dodge Zone Manager there, Leo Desmond, had been his father's friend in Janesville. Mr. Desmond was pleased to visit with him and inquired about his father. He stated that reorganization was taking place and he was not able to hire any employees at this time.

Holt made his next stop at the Buick Motor Division Zone Office in Chicago. Bob Mason, Office Manager, greeted him and took his application. Jim Hudgens, Zone Manager, reviewed the application, and told

Mason, "This man doesn't have the qualifications to work for Buick."

Holt then traveled to Cincinnati to apply at the Nash Zone Office. He was greeted warmly and renewed acquaintances with several people whom he had worked with while in Columbus, Indiana. The Zone Manager was not available, so he was asked to return and make his application in two days.

Not wanting to waste time, he proceeded to go to 3rd and Walnut St. in Cincinnati, where General Motors had offices for Buick, Pontiac, and Olds. Buick was on the seventh floor. He was greeted by Lenard Dallow, Office Manager, who took his application. Glenn Wilson, the Zone Manager invited him into his office and reviewed the application. He asked several questions, then asked Holt to call him at one o'clock. Holt departed, spent some time walking around downtown Cincinnati, and called Wilson at the proper time.

He was informed that he was to be in Detroit, Michigan the following Tuesday to meet with Mr. Jim Bradshaw, Central Regional Manager, who would make the decision on his employment.

The meeting took place with Bradshaw in late September. Holt received a phone call from Wilson the next day, and told to report to him October 1st. Holt began his employ-

Paul, about 1956.

Louise in 1955.

ment with Buick Motor Division as the District Manager of District #2, Dayton, Ohio.

His first week was spent with C.L. "Chuck" Foster, who was the former District Manager of that District. Chuck was being given District #1, City Manager of Cincinnati. He was an enthusiastic employee, and every dealer we contacted spoke highly of him.

The two worked well together during the ten days they contacted the dealers of District #2. The Dayton District consisted of thirty-one dealers from Chillicothe, Ohio to Connersville, Indiana and north to Sidney, Ohio then south to Middletown, Ohio. Principal dealer points were two metropolitan dealers

in Dayton/Springfield, Ohio and Richmond, Indiana. This was a strong District, as many General Motors plants were located in the area. Holt served this area for almost two years and then was transferred to Indianapolis District #6.

The Buick dealer in Eaton, Ohio was Anthony "Tony" Lampe. Since he had been a former roadman with Buick and was a newly appointed dealer, he knew Holt's job, and Holt knew the problems dealers had. The two helped each other and became lifetime friends.

On June 11, 1954, Lampe's wife, Bernadine, arranged a blind date for Holt with Lou-

The color photo below right was taken as they left the Church of the Brethern, Eaton, Ohio on their wedding day, as they were on the way to Eaton Country Club for the reception. After a brief stop at the Miller home, they departed for a trip to Niagara Falls, New York. The trip was shortened, since Holt had to return to Flint and attend a black tie dinner given for Ivan Wiles, who had been promoted to Central Office, Detroit. All sales department, central office staff, and Zone Managers nationwide were expected to attend. It was held at the Durant Hotel on March 31st, 1956.

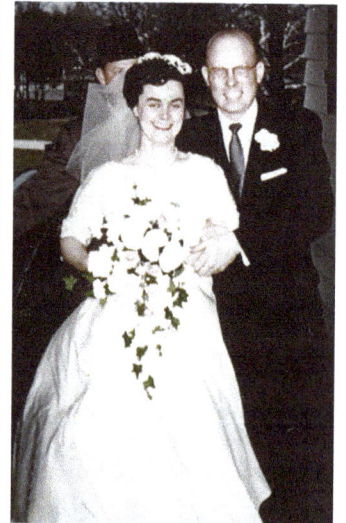

ise Miller. The two couples attended the horse races at the Preble County Fair Grounds. This started the courtship that resulted in their marriage on March 25, 1956.

In the spring of 1954, Holt was transferred to District #6, Indianapolis, Indiana. Having served with his father at the Nash Dealership in Columbus, Indiana, he felt he knew the area and several of the dealers. Buick market penetration in the District was poor and Buick wanted improvement. The dealership in Anderson was changed and the incoming dealer was a strong addition.

Bill Curry was appointed the Zone Manager in Cincinnati, and his father owned and operated the dealership in Bloomington, Indiana. Holt was told that Buick wanted a third dealer in Indianapolis, so he proceeded to contact several dealers he knew there.

Forrest Ripley, the dealer in Springfield, Ohio (Holt's former District) had a son who was selected and appointed the third metropolitan dealer. Holt suggested that Plainfield, Indiana was a growing area that could cover west Indianapolis and Speedway. "Red" Dillon was appointed to Plainfield. Dillon was a former Used Car Manager for an Indianapolis Oldsmobile dealer. He was young, enthusiastic, and under-capitalized, but more than made up for it by hard work.

These changes in late 1954 set the stage for a robust 1955. With the market exploding in 1955, Indianapolis began to be considered as a possible new Zone. Holt was not informed of this until late November, when Robert Blair, newly appointed Regional Manager, came to Indianapolis and asked to see what offices he had selected. Holt was "floored." He had not been informed but did not want to reveal this, as this might reflect badly on his Zone Manager, Curry.

Holt drove Blair around the city, showing him the major office complexes, then took him to the airport so he could catch the flight back to Detroit. The following day, Holt contacted the Zone and asked if he should survey the area for office space. He was told that it was being handled by ARGANOT (G.M. Real estate department) and to keep this information to himself. Indianapolis was made a new Zone on January 1, 1956.

Paul Britton, former Assistant Zone Manager in Cincinnati, was appointed the Zone Manager in Indianapolis. Holt received a telephone call from Britton, telling him to report to the new Zone office at four o'clock on Friday afternoon. Not knowing what was is store for him, Holt reported as directed. Britton call him into his office, and informed him he was being transferred to Home Office in Flint, Michigan. He was directed to report to Glenn Wilson, newly appointed Director of Merchandising, Monday morning at eight. He was instructed to take a flight Sunday and a room would be assigned at the Durant Hotel, Sunday night.

Holt reported to his former Zone Manager, Glenn Wilson, as directed. He was also greeted by Jim Bradshaw, who was now Assistant Sales Manager, home office. Wilson told him that he would be an assistant merchandising specialist, reporting to Dick Cogswell, Sales Promotion Manager, and working with Lyle Carpenter, who was also an assistant merchandising specialist.

The entire Sales Staff at Home Office consisted of only eight men who directed the entire Division. Al Belfie, General Sales Manager; Jim Bradshaw, Assistant Sales Manager; Glenn Wilson, Director of Merchandising; Dick Cogswell, Sales Promotion Manager, Jim Graham, Advertising Manager, Roy Federson, Show Manager, Lyle Carpenter, and Paul Holt. Out of all these men, only two had ever sold cars at retail — Wilson and Holt.

This was an unexpected move, but Holt looked forward to being at the center of the Division. The move had its drawbacks, too. Since he was now assigned to Home Office, his road car was removed. And, since he was not traveling, the expense account was not used. Suppliers and the Advertising agency, Kudner, were always available, to invite us to lunch, though.

Holt remarked to Wilson, after being given a $50.00 raise that he didn't know how long he could afford "all this prosperity." Wilson replied, "Get used to it!" and they both laughed.

It was during this period that Holt began to learn about the rich history of Buick Division. Things like the Durant Hotel was named after William Crapo Durant, who brought Buick to Flint from Detroit and used Buick as the cornerstone in the formation of General Motors, and about General Managers of the Division, such as Charles Nash and Walter Chrysler who formed their own companies. He also learned that the current President of General Motors, Harlow H. Curtice, rescued Buick from the depths of depression in the 1930s. Even though he was President of General Motors, he closely followed the events at Buick, as a father looks after his children.

Harlow Curtice was born August 15, 1893 in Petrieville, Michigan, near Flint. He studied accounting at Ferris College, graduating in 1914. His first job was with Standard Rule Company. When the company was sold, he joined General Motors AC Spark Plug Division around June 1914. One year later, he was made comptroller of AC, at the age of twenty-one. He served in the Army in World War I, and returned to AC Spark Plug Division in 1923. He became General Manager of AC Division in 1929. Alfred Sloan was looking for a manager to revitalize Buick Division, and since Curtice had proven himself at AC, he was appointed General Manager of Buick in late 1933.

Buick's sales of the 1933 model were 40,620. Curtice revised the model line-up, by introducing Model 40. By sharing tooling cost with Chevrolet, he was able to lower the cost of this new model to under $1,000. Sales took off, even during the depression. Model year sales increased to 78,757 in 1934. Each year, thereafter, sales increased, proving the leadership of Harlow H. Curtice had revitalized Buick Division. In late 1940, Curtice offered Buick's entire production to William S. Knudsen, former President of General Motors, and now Director of the National Defense Advisory Board.

Achievements Buick made during World War II include: producing 74,797 Pratt & Whitney aircraft engines, developing and producing the M-18 Hellcat Tank Destroyer, and producing over one billion dollars of War Materials at reduced prices, on time and ahead of schedule.

These achievements increased the legacy of Curtice, and he was named President of General Motors on February 2, 1953. He led the firm to its greatest heights in 1955, commanding slightly more than 52% of all domestic automobile sales that year. His comment, "What is good for General Motors is good for our Country," earned him the *Time Magazine* Man of the Year award in 1955.

Holt had contact with Harlow Curtice on two occasions when he was employed at Buick. In October of 1955, all field personnel, a little less than six hundred men, from all corners of America, came to Flint for their annual new car announcement meeting. On Monday morning at eight o'clock, we were ordered to report to the I.M.A. Building. Greeting us at the entrance were three men: Ivan Wiles, General Manager; Al Belfie, General Sales Manager; and Harlow Curtice, President of General Motors. They shook the hands of every man that entered the building.

It was unprecedented to have the President of General Motors at a new car announcement meeting. Curtice was the first speaker that morning. Everyone there surely remembers his comments. He started by saying "Gentlemen, I have come here to congratulate you on your achievements last year. Buick sold 786,000 units last year, the largest volume in its history. You moved Buick into third place in sales, behind Chevrolet and Ford, accounting for 10.3% of all domestic sales. But before you become overconvenient with this record, remember you still lost nine out of every ten sales last year."

There was a moan throughout the audience, then laughter, and finally every one clapped and cheered. This was typical of Curtice. He had the ability to verbally chastise his subordinates, which made them work even harder beyond their capacity.

G.M. economists had forecasted a decline in domestic sales for 1956. To make sure sales would not fall as far as they had predicted, each Division was ordered to institute sales incentives. Buick chose to create a Dealer-Salesman Contest, where points would be earned with each new unit sold. These points would be redeemed for prizes selected from a catalog. The program was organized by Reynolds and Reynolds from Dayton, Ohio.

Zone Managers were invited to Flint in mid-February for the announcement of the program. At a dinner attended by Curtice, Wiles, Belifie, all Zone Managers and

The 1956 Merchandising Department of Buick is pictured above, dressed as Buccaneers which was the theme of the program. Pictured left to right are: Dick Cogswell, Sales Promotion Manager; Lyle Carpenter, Merchandising Assistant; Glenn Wilson, Director of Merchandising; Jim Graham, Advertising Manager; and Paul Holt, Merchandising Assistant. Roy Federson was not showen, as he was on assignment.

Regional Managers, as well as Department Managers, the program was presented, in the main dinning room of the Durant Hotel.

The contest ran from March through April and was a success, but did not stop the sales decline as hoped. Model year sales declined to under 440,000 units, a decline of almost 45%. A decline like this caused dealers' profits to vanish. When this happens, Dealers become unhappy and tend to seek solutions.

Because of this discontent, Dealer Councils were formed in all Divisions. Twelve dealers from each Zone were elected to discuss problems with Zone Officials. From these meetings, two Dealers were selected to attend a Regional Meeting and meet with the Regional Officials. Two Dealers were selected from each of the six Regional Meetings and these twelve Dealers were invited to attend a meeting in Flint with the General Manager and General Sales Manager.

There was a great deal of uncertainty about this first Dealer Council Meeting in home office. Buick was determined that it would go off without problems. Jim Hudgens, newly appointed Assistant General Sales Manager, called a meeting with the merchandising department and gave assignments to each of us: hotel assignments, banner for the front door, and transportation. At the end of the meeting, Hudgens expressed a desire that everything go off with precision, and then asked if anyone had anything to add.

Holt replied, "Ask Bob Mason (Organization Manager) to go through the dealers' files and find out the date each of these twelve dealers signed their first Buick Contract, also get their birthdays. If any of these dates come up during the dinners, have Ragsdale and Kennard present them with a cake." Hudgens said that was a good idea and he would mention it to Kennard. Holt was later informed that a dealer had a birthday, and was presented with a cake. This seemed to be the point at which Dealers became more willing to work with Management and lost their antagonistic attitude.

The first Dealer Council Meeting was deemed a success at Buick. One of the Dealer ideas that came out of the meetings was to eliminate the Dealer Advertising Accounts and permit each dealer to handle his own advertising. Prior to this, each dealer was billed $35 per car and the factory matched this amount. Dealers were permitted to use this money for road signs and local radio advertising, but the bulk of the money was spent on local newspaper ads.

Al Belfie had been appointed Director of Merchandising for the Corporation. He was concerned that the refunds of the dealer portions of the funds would exceed the amounts left in each dealer's fund, thus requiring an appropriation from the Corporation. He set up a series of meetings with each Division.

Because he still lived in Flint, Buick was the first meeting. At the meeting, attended by Kennard Hudgens, Glenn Wilson, and Paul Holt, Belfle asked Wilson how much money would be left after Dealers were paid. Wilson had not anticipated this and was giving the reasons why the amount would vary due to charges and contributions.

Seeing his boss was not giving what Belfie wanted, Holt responded; "Mr. Belfie, there will be $735,000 in the account after all 3,200 dealers are paid."

Belfie glared at Holt and said, "How sure are you about that sum?"

Holt responded, "Mr. Belfie, if I miss my estimate by more than 5%, then I guess there will be a new man in the Mail Room next month."

Belfie smiled and said, "You can count on it."

In the following three weeks, Holt kept checking on production, which remained as forecasted, so income to the fund was maintained. At the beginning of the fourth week, Wilson stopped by Holt's office and said, "Bolton (Comptroller) just called me to report there was $751,000 in the account after Dealers were paid."

Holt smiled and said, "Great! Looks like you will have to put up with me for a few more months."

Sales continue to decline for the 1956 model. Everyone was concerned with the announcement of the 1957 model, seeking a rebound in sales. Corporation was also concerned, and Harlow Curtice secured an appropriation for Buick of five million dollars to accelerate sales.

It was decided, by Ragsdale and Kennard, with some direction from Curtice and Belfie, to launch the largest newspaper ad campaign in automobile history — three ads a week for thirteen weeks in the eighty largest metropolitan cities in America. These were to be hard-hitting price ads, with the largest ads to be 1,500 lines (three-quarters of a page) and the smallest ad to be 840 lines (a quarter of a page). The cost of these ads would be four million dollars. The other million would be spent on a Dealer-Salesman Prize Contest. The ads and contest would begin mid-February and last until mid May.

The ads were designed by Kudner Advertising Agency, presented to Ragsdale and Kennard for approval, then sent to Wilson and Holt for processing and final approval. Since these were all price ads, it was important that each ad specify what accessories would be standard and extras, like white wall tires, be noted in the disclaimer. Of the thirty-nine ads, only one contained a disclaimer that bothered Holt. The disclaimer stated: "Including Dynaflow, Power Steering, Power Brakes, AM-FM Radio and White Wall Tires." The ad should have read *excluding* Dynaflow, Power Steering, Power Brakes, AM-FM Radio and White Wall Tires". Holt called this to Wilson's attention, and the agency admitted the error and changed the ad.

Wilson latter told Holt, "You saved the Division several million dollars, because Buick would have honored anything it put in print."

The spring selling season for the 1957 model did not go as well as management had hoped. By mid-year, it was easy to see that Buick would have another loss in volume. Harlow Curtice, Tony De Lorenzo (Public Relation Manager for GM) and Al Belfie all retained their homes in Flint and became weekend visitors to the executives at Flint.

One weekend, Curtice called a meeting for the entire Sales Staff to meet for lunch at the City Club. The City Club was on the sixteenth floor of the Durant Hotel and was one of Curtice's favorite dinning establishments. Wilson, Carpenter, and Holt arrived to find Curtice, De Lorenzo, and Belfie seated on the couch, with Bolton (Comptroller) and Kennard sitting on one side of the couch and Ragsdale sitting at the other end of the couch.

Waldo McNaught and Jerry Rideout (Buick Public Relations) stood behind the couch.

As Wilson, Holt and Carpenter stood facing the couch, Curtice began the informal meeting by stating he had to report to the GM Board on Monday and he needed reasons why sales performance had not met established goals. Ragsdale (General Manager) was taking most of the heat and was nervously trying to reply to Curtice.

Everyone remained silent while Curtice unloaded his displeasure about the sales performance. It was then Al Belfie spoke up and said, "Mr. Curtice, Buick Sales this model year will be under 330,000 units, and we will not retake third place in domestic sales, but our market share loss was less than other Divisions. We spent the five million appropriation you approved as wisely as we could, with the largest newspaper ad campaign in the industry. I only have one point to make. *Where would we be if we hadn't spent the money?*"

There was complete silence, then Curtice smiled and said, "You're right Al. Come on, let's have lunch." Curtice had his reply to the Board.

The most important lesson Holt learned while working at the main office was given to him by Ed Kennard. With the sales decline at Buick, everyone at home office was inclined to be a little on edge. One morning, while

Holt was reviewing schedules in Wilson's office, Kennard entered in a rush. He had just left Ragsdale's office and was in a rush to return. Kennard outlined an idea for a dealer program that Ragsdale had proposed. He told Wilson and Holt to put together this promotion, type it up and have it on his desk by two o'clock. He then left to return to his office to handle other matters.

Wilson and Holt were stunned, because they knew dealers would not buy into a program like Kennard had outlined. They spent twenty to thirty minutes trying to revise it and make it a program Dealers would buy into that still contained Ragsdale's main point.

Kennard came out of his office, saw Wilson and Holt and knew the dilemma each of them was experiencing. Kennard entered Wilson's office and said, "Look, it doesn't matter what each of us wants. This is the way the Boss wants it, so get busy, put it together and have it on my desk by two."

Both agreed, outlined the program, reviewed it, and with minor changes gave it to Wilson's secretary to type. The program was put into effect and was not accepted by most of the dealers. Holt learned this: It doesn't make any difference how good your ideals are — don't express them unless asked. If you are directed by a superior to carry out

a project, do it the way he tells you with no deviation.

Waldo McNaught had been selected by Tony De Lorenzo to succeed him as Public Relations Director of Buick. When Curtice was appointed President in 1953, De Lorenzo went with Curtice to the Corporation as Director of Public Relations for the Corporation.

Waldo had been a newspaper man throughout his life, but adapted well to his new responsibilities. Everyone liked and respected Waldo. He had only two assistants, Jerry Rideout and Helen Turrey, his secretary. Whenever he needed manpower, Waldo would call on the merchandising department to assist his staff.

Waldo was a member of Warwick Hills Realty, which sold residential lots in an exclusive section south of Flint. One day, Chuck Kelley approached Waldo and asked him to build a golf course. Waldo wrote letters to a number of prominent people, and around seventy-five people joined at the initial cost of two thousand dollars each. The Country Club and golf course were completed in 1956.

Waldo had an idea that would promote the sale of residential lots and help Buick get national recognition, so he brought the subject up at a dinner attended by Ragsdale, Curtice, and De Lorenzo. He asked, "Why not promote a PGA Golf Tournament at Warwick Hills and call it the Buick Open?"

Ragsdale was not a golfer and was against the idea, fearing the expense involved. Waldo assured Ragsdale there would be no cost to Buick, as he could raise the money from outside sources. Curtice liked the idea, as no other Automotive Company had such an event. Waldo was given permission to go ahead.

Waldo made contact with the PGA representatives, and invited them to Flint to look over the course. After looking over the course, they were not inclined to schedule a national tournament there. That was when Waldo made the offer of a $50,000 award to the winner. This amount was the largest purse offered for any PGA tournament at the time. The representatives willingly agreed to schedule Warwick Hills as the Buick Open.

Waldo had an okay from Buick, as long as no expense was incurred by Buick, but had just offered $50,000 to the PGA. So, he had his work cut out for him. He secured the funds he needed by developing a program and selling ads to Buick's suppliers. Other revenues were developed by charging admission and parking fees. Buick employees were charged only $1.00 admission. Waldo was able to raise more than enough money to cover his expenses, including the banquet dinner held after the tournament.

The Merchandising Department was very active. Carpenter and Holt handled the tally board. Scores were relayed by mobile phones and posted promptly. Cogswell and Graham drove golf carts loaded with drinks and towels. It was a very busy four days.

The first Buick Open took place in the summer of 1956, and it became an annual event that lasted until 2007. It all came about because of Waldo McNaught.

The development of the 1959 Models gave Buick hope for resurgence in sales. In the spring of 1958, rumors began about a change in Advertising Agency. Holt continued to work with Kudner Advertising and was not involved with the selection. Both Kennard and Ragsdale were seeking a fresh new approach to the market, and it was certain that a new Agency could provide this, if the *right* Agency was selected.

It wasn't until Kennard brought in a contract from McCann-Erickson Advertising that Holt knew there would be a change. Kennard explained that GM Legal had reviewed it, and ask Holt to look it over to see if he saw anything they should be aware of. Kennard expressly stated that *no one* should be advised of the selection.

Holt reviewed the contract and returned it to Kennard with only a small suggestion as to the Agency's commission. McCann-Erickson took over as Buick's new Advertising Agency officially on July 1st, 1958. However, internally we worked with two Agencies most of the spring of 1958.

Rumors of Ragsdale's replacement began to surface at this time, as well as whispers about Curtice's retirement. This led to more uncertainty on the second floor of Buick's headquarters.

Verne Mathews, Chief Engineer of Buick, had worked for the Corporation most of his life. He retired in early 1958. It was customary when a Department Head retired to have a farewell dinner, and all executives were expected to attend.

Holt recalls that at the gathering before dinner Vern was asked, "Now that you have retired, where are you going and what do you intend on doing?" Vern replied that he and his wife had purchased a nice home in Florida, and the mortgage would not be a problem. He planned on doing a lot of fishing.

The next day, Holt was in Car Distribution, and someone mentioned that Verne Mathews had ordered his retirement car — a Skylark Sedan with standard transmission, air conditioning and nothing else. This was a man who had always driven Roadmasters with every possible option, as long has he worked for Buick. Now he wanted a stripped-down basic model?

Holt began to wonder if the retirement General Motors was offering would place him in a similar position in thirty years. Holt remembered the many moves his father and mother had made and the disruption in his early education. This caused him to question whether he wanted to subject his family to this.

By mid-summer of 1958, the stress of working with two Agencies and preparing for the new model (the redesigning of the entire model line-up) and the worry of being shuffled around the country, caused him to submit his resignation on July 5th, effective July 20th.

That weekend, he took his pregnant wife and one-year-old son to Henry Ford Museum in Detroit, and relaxed for the first time in months. Holt was given a farewell luncheon in Flint and he bid goodbye to all of his associates.

When news of his departure was public, he received notice from Dodge Division, American Motors, and Grey Advertising Agency. Jack Minor, General Manager of Dodge, interviewed him. A supplier friend of Holt's advised him that there were things going on at Dodge that were not right, and to stay away. Holt later learned that Minor's son-in-law was hired as Advertising Manager.

Grey Advertising Agency flew Holt to New York for interview and psychological tests. He was later informed that an opening would come up in Washington, and he was being considered for that position.

Roy Abernathy, General Sales Manager of American Motors interviewed Holt and offered him two dealer points, Sandusky, Ohio and Hamilton, Ohio. Holt agreed to look at both areas. Sandusky, Ohio was very much a summer resort area, which would mean a large volume of business in the summer and very little volume in winter. Hamilton, Ohio was supported by three main businesses, and Holt's friend, Ed Larkin, had successfully operated in that city for many years. Also, it was twenty miles south of his wife's home.

Holt knew many of the dealers in the area, as he had traveled that area when he was District Manager with Buick. Hamilton, Ohio was selected and he became the American Motors dealer on Oct 10, 1958, exactly ten years after his father became a Nash Dealer in Indiana.

The first year of business, 159 new units were sold, which was three times more than the previous dealer had sold. What was more important was that 269 used cars were sold. Sales volume could have been greater, but American Motors had failed to cancel a small satellite dealer nine miles away in a crossroad called Millville. This caused a major change in the future plans Holt had for the agency. New facilities were put on hold and expansion was

cancelled. While the business remained profitable, it was not what Holt had hoped.

When American Motors pressed for a new facility, Holt would not agree until American Motors honored their agreement to remove the Millville site. The Franchise was terminated in October 1961.

Holt found himself with his wife expecting their third child, plus two young boys and 40 used cars, not to mention a modest home, with a mortgage. A realtor offered a nice location for a used car outlet, which Holt purchased. So, Holt became a Used Car Dealer at 795 South Erie in Hamilton.

Without a franchise, this business became a struggle, and this was not what he wanted. At this time, Roy Federson called him and invited him to lunch in Cincinnati, and Holt's life began to change. Roy had just been appointed Assistant Zone Manager at the Buick Zone in Cincinnati.

The old friends hadn't had contact for seven years, and the meeting was happy reunion. Roy ended the luncheon with the statement, "We have to get you in a Buick Deal!" Thus began Holt's series of trips to potential dealer points.

In the fall of 1970, Holt was advised that Scottie Shackro of New Carlisle, Ohio had died on a hunting trip. Shackro had been a dealer Holt had called on when he traveled the Dayton area, and he'd also purchased

used cars from him to supply his lot in Hamilton. A meeting was arranged with Paul Shakro, Scottie's brother, and an agreement was worked out which would transfer the dealership to Holt.

The first day of operation was November 26, 1969. General Motors had been on strike, and only two new cars were in stock. Holt looked at the prices of those two cars — A LeSabre at $5,300 and a Special at $5,100 — and was shocked. He had not sold any new Ramblers for more than $2,700. So, he was apprehensive about the financial move he had just made.

His first customer was Darrel Burson, who bought the LeSabre. Darrel later became Holt's next-door neighbor, and remained a life-long friend.

Holt Buick-GMC was profitable from its first day, and although it was never a large dealership, it provided a suitable income for the Holt family. Holt's three children, Paul, Jim and Mary all progressed through the local school system and graduated from Tecumseh High School. All three attended college.

The public is inclined to think all automobile dealers are wealthy. They see several dozen new cars on the lot with five-digit dollar signs and an impressive showroom, and just make that assumption. The truth is, they are highly leveraged. Those new cars on the lot are owned by a finance firm, even those he holds a title to in his business name. Those finance firms (GMAC, Chrysler Credit, CIT, to name a few) are very firm about enforcing their rules. Dealers are required to pay off the indebtedness within twenty-four hours of delivery of a new car. Since most sales involve trades, a dealer normally does not receive enough money to payoff the new car.

Holt remembers his first encounter on this subject with GMAC. He had been a dealer for about two months, and three special order cars arrived in the middle of the week. Arrangements were made to deliver those cars on the weekend. Sales from walk-

Paul and Louise with their three children, Paul, Jim and Mary.

ins accounted for four additional cars. On Friday, he delivered three cars and on Saturday he delivered four cars. So, on Monday morning he sent GMAC a check for the seven cars.

Tuesday morning, about ten o'clock, a sedan pulled up in front of the dealership and four men bounded out of the car. Two proceeded to new car lot across the street. Holt greeted John Williams, the GMAC Manager,

105

Paul and Louise with their children, December 1971.

at the door. The other man went to his office and demanded to see the titles.

Holt could tell John was upset, so he asked if he could help him. *"You paid off seven cars yesterday!"* John shouted.

Holt replied, "Yes we did. We had a great weekend."

John, still upset, stated, "This dealership has never sold that many cars in a weekend. Let me see your bank deposits and your receipt book."

Holt produced the requested items. Shortly, one of the men, who had been across the street checking the inventory, came in and reported to Williams, "They're all here."

John spent about twenty minutes reviewing the deposits and receipts. He finally looked at Holt and with a stunned expression on his face said, *"You sold seven cars last weekend!"*

Holt replied, "That's what I told you, John. This isn't Shackro Buick anymore."

John Williams went on to explain that he would have to write a report to Detroit explaining that Holt was not "floating cars." He explained that if this ever happened again,

Holt was to pay-off three cars, and then the next day he should pay-off the remaining four cars. Holt explained that he had only been following the rules of GMAC.

Holt learned that the supervision of an Automobile Finance Company can be intense and dictatorial, because they usually have more money at stake than the dealer.

In December 1981, Holt received a letter advising him that General Motors desired to combine the Pontiac GMC and Buick agencies. Holt contacted the Pontiac dealer, who stated he did not want to sell and was not interested in adding the Buick agency. Holt reported back to his Buick Zone Office and was told, "Just sit tight, he will come around."

Four years later, the Pontiac dealer and Holt signed a "buy-sell" agreement. In January 1985, the two dealers met in the Pontiac Zone Office and were told that Pontiac would not agree to the merger. Since both dealers had received similar letters from GM, they were confused and disappointed.

At this point, Holt made up his mind that if the merger was not acceptable, he would sell to anyone who would pay a fair price. A young salesman from Troy contacted Holt, and Charles D. Stapleton purchased Holt Buick-GMC Inc. on October 18, 1989.

Holt looked at several dealerships in the area, but the economy was soft, and the prices were out of line with the marketing

Paul and Louise on their 45th wedding anniversary.

Paul and Louise in 2012.

107

Louise and Paul Holt in Mendocino, Calif. in 2001.

areas. Holt was contacted by an old friend, Travis Tefft, who connected him with A-Plus Car Rental of Salisbury NC. He was offered the State of Ohio, but this later changed to the western half of Ohio. It permitted Holt to contact his friends in the Automobile business, and kept him busy. The business suffered many changes, but was finally sold to an insurance company and continues today as U.S. Choice Auto Rental.

On the 40th Anniversary of their wedding, Louise and Paul decided to visit Hawaii. This eleven-day trip included a visit with Louise's High School classmate, Jackie R. Grove. Since Jackie was married to a former Air Force Officer, he took us on a tour of the island and showed us Hickman Field, where most of the Air Force aircraft were destroyed during the Japanese attack on Dec 7, 1941. Many of the buildings still had bullet holes from the Japanese attack.

Like most tourists, we also visited the Battleship Arizona. Paul and Louise then rejoined the Globus Group for the five-island tour.

The family gathered June 16th in Gatlinburg Tennessee and proceeded to the "Black Bear Dinner Show." The following morning they gathered for breakfast at Bennets. The grandchildren were given expense money and released to enjoy the events of the park.

That evening we gathered at "Dolly Parton's Dixie Dinner and Show. On Sunday morning, we gathered at the entrance of Gatlinburg at a pancake house for breakfast. We departed about noon to return home. It was a weekend enjoyed and remembered by all, especially Paul and Louise Holt.

Paul Holt never ran for public office, however he was always interested in the betterment of the communities where he had businesses. He was asked to join Lions International, a business service club, while working for his father in Columbus, Indiana. In April 1949, he accepted this invitation. When he returned to the University of Wisconsin, in the fall of 1950, he was unable to continue his membership. He joined Buick Motor Division, after completing his degree on Oct. 1ˢᵗ, 1952, and was unable to rejoin the Lions as he was traveling as a road man, and on call by the Division.

Proud grandparents Louise (Miller) Holt and Paul L. Holt with grandson Chris Bubier in December of 2002.

In Oct 1958, he became the Rambler Dealer in Hamilton, Ohio and rejoined the Lions. He served as President of the Hamilton Club in 1968. He also served as President of the New Carlisle Lions Club, as well as the Troy, Ohio Lions Club, twice. He was honored by the Troy Club with the Melvin Johns Fellowship award in 2011. He has maintained perfect attendance for over fifty years.

After he sold his dealership in October 1989, he was appointed to the Planning and Zoning Board of New Carlisle by the Mayor of New Carlisle. He served on this Board for five years, the last two as Chairman. This was the only public office he ever held.

Paul Holt joined the Lions International in March 1949 in Columbus, Indiana. He left this club to attend the University of Wisconsin to continue his degree. Rules were different then. You could not be more than 35 years old, and there could be no more than two members in the same employment. Women were not permitted membership.

It was not possible to study and attend meetings and activites. After joining Buick,

he was driving all day and writing reports in the evening. He rreturned to the Lions when he settled in Hamilton, in November 1958.

The family gathered in Gatlinburg, Tennessee on the 50th wedding anniversary of Paul And Louise Holt. Back row, left to right: James Holt, Michael Bubier, Paul L. Holt, Paul C. Holt, Alex Holt, Andy Holt. Middle row: Mary Holt Bubier, Linda Darling Holt. Bottom row: Christopher Bubier, Laurie Holt, Louise Miller Holt, Liza Holt, and Marianne Holt

He transferred to New Carlisle, Ohio in Dec. 1970, and then to Troy, Ohio in Dec.1998. He earned the 50 year perfect attendance pin in 2011. He was awarded the Melvin Jones Fellowship award in Troy, Ohio. He still keeps in touch with friends he made in Lions and with "pin traders."

PAUL CLAYTON HOLT

Born: February 22, 1957, Flint, Michigan

Married: Linda Darling, Lakeland, Florida, Aug. 4, 2001

Died:

Interment:

Paul began elementary school in Hamilton, Ohio. His family moved to New Carlisle, Ohio when his father took the Buick franchise in New Carlisle. He was a member of the baseball team and played trumpet in the high school concert and marching bands.

After high school, he entered The Ohio State University in the fall of 1975 and earned a Bachelor's degree in finance in 1979, and went on to earn an MBA from the University of Wisconsin-Madison in 1980.

In the fall of 1980, he was employed by CIT Group, a consumer finance company. Later, he became employed by Chrysler First Wholesale Credit and later world Omni Finance in the 1980s and early 1990s.

Wanting to take a break from the business world, he applied and was accepted into AmeriCorps. He was assigned as a counselor at a Salvation Army homeless shelter in Champaign, Illinois. He was later hired by the Salvation Army as an employee serving in the same function.

At left, Paul and James on Labor Day in 1961. Above, Paul, Mary and James in 1965.

Paul at high school graduation in 1975.

After three years, he returned to his parents' home in Troy, Ohio. While in Troy, he contacted his old friend from high school, Darryl Bauer, and they attended the high school class of 1975's reunion.

Paul remembered a girl he dated at Ohio State University. He found that she had moved to Lakeland, Florida and was employed as a Nurse Practitioner. Paul flew to Lakeland, Florida for a visit. He then brought Linda to Troy to meet his parents. Wedding plans were made and they were married on August 4, 2001.

They were blessed with a daughter, Marianne Elizabeth Holt on, on July 27, 2004.

In 2003, Paul found employment in Lakeland as a national accounts manager with the nation's largest independent automotive tool & equipment specialist, serving wholesalers and distributors throughout North America.

This photo was taken in Troy, Ohio on day we first met Linda.

Paul and Linda on their wedding day, August 4, 2001.

Paul and her dog in 2002.

113

Linda with her mother, Francis Darling.

Paul has attended several National Auto Dealers Conventions, displaying product for this company. The picture below was taken in 2014 National Convention when Ford announced the new all aluminum F-1500. This truck required several special tools to repair the aluminum body, which Paul's firm supplied.

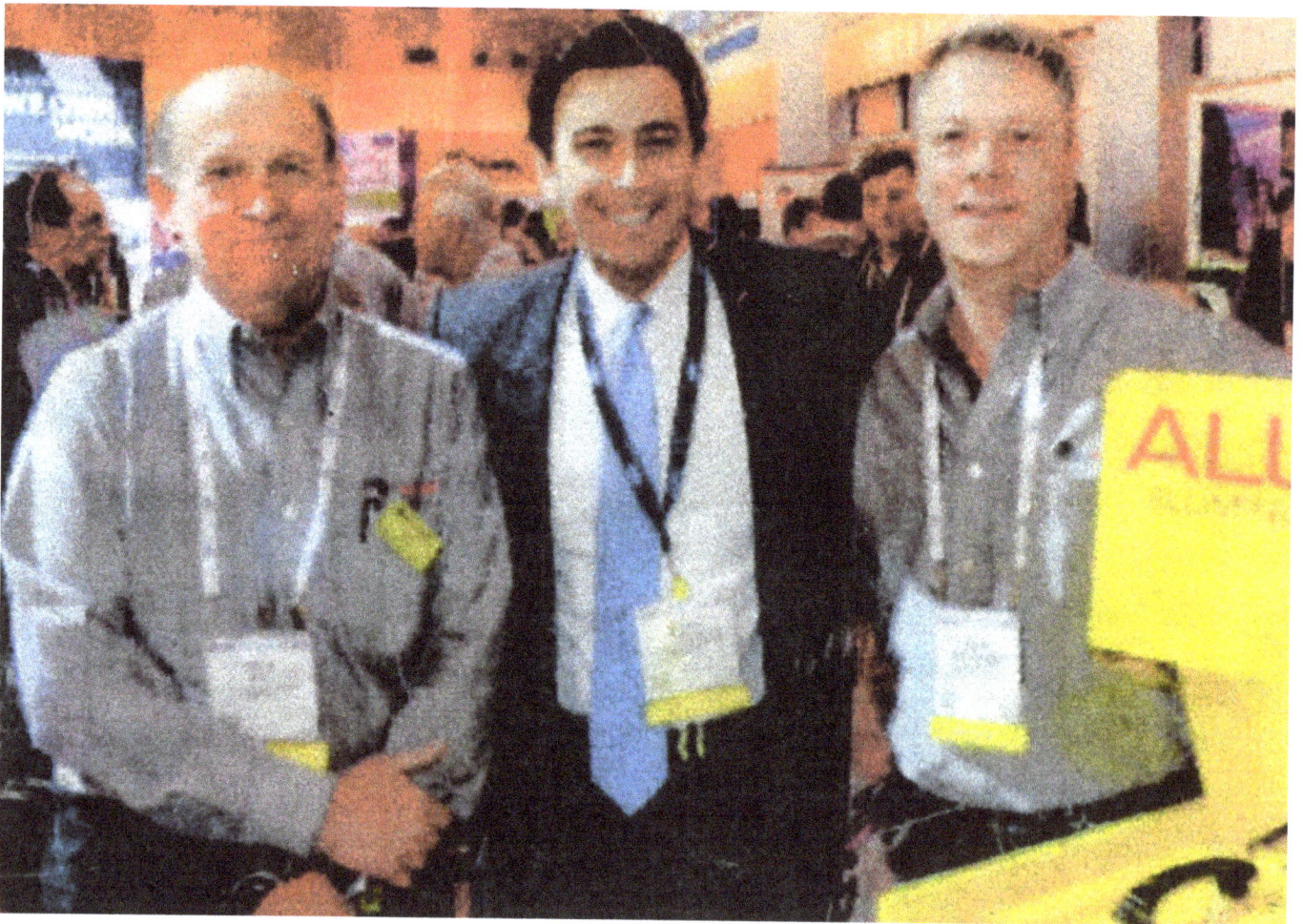

Paul on the left with Mark Fields, newly appointed CEO of Ford Motor Company. The sales representative on the right represents Dentfix Company, also a specialty tool company.

Marianne at 13 months.

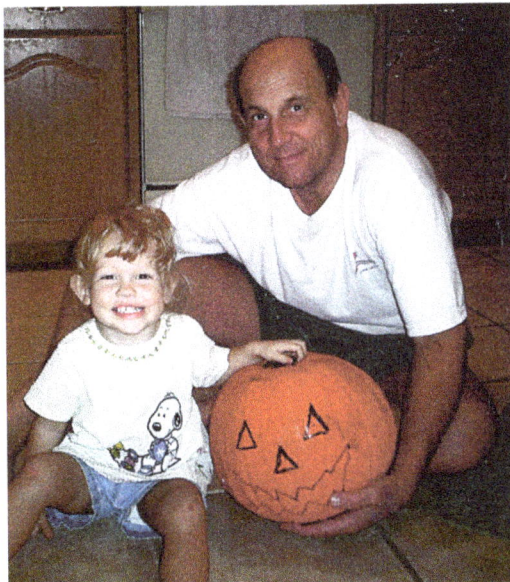

Paul with Marianne, Nov. 2006.

Paul C. Holt, son of Paul Jr., with his daughter, Marianne.

Marianne began her music instruction at the age of ten. Her father, Paul, worked with her and she was able to join her Middle School Jazz Band when she was eleven.

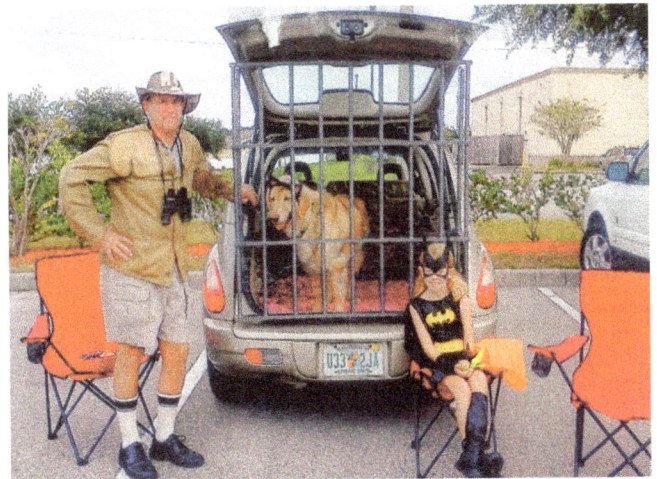

She was chosen to play in the Polk County All County Band. She was accepted at Harrison School of the Arts, Lakeland, Fla., in the fall of 2018, when she began High School.

JAMES LAWRENCE HOLT

Born: September 14, 1958, Hamilton, Ohio

Married: Georgia Rinaldi, July 13, 1980. Divorced April 2, 2001.
                Engaged to Brooke Tweddell, December 25, 2013.

Died:

Interment:

James is the second son of Paul and Louise M. Holt. He began his education in the elementary schools of Fairfield, Ohio. He was a good student and became a member of the High School Wrestling Team. He graduated from Tecumseh High School, New Carlisle, Ohio in 1976. His High School graduation picture is on the following page.

He wanted to remain in the Automobile business with his father, but his father suggested that he go to college to broaden his background. He chose to go to Ohio University, since it offered an individualized study program with a two-year degree. Jim became very active on campus and was Advertising Manager for the campus newspaper. He also chaired the Pop Concert Committee and joined Delta Tau Fraternity.

His activity with the Pop Concert Committee became more important as he arranged Concerts with Bob Hope, Billy Joel, and other big name stars.

Tecumseh High School graduation photo.

While working at the university newspaper, he met a young, attractive girl named Georgia Rinaldi. They began dating and this union resulted in their marriage on July 13, 1980, in Glenn Ridge, New Jersey.

In the summer of 1979, he began his search for employment with a concert promoter. That same year, he accepted a position as Promotion and Production Manager with Mid-South Concerts in Memphis, Tennessee. He worked for Bob Kelley for fourteen years and was elevated to Vice President of the company.

While at Mid-South Concerts Jim negotiated a partnership agreement with Memphis in May International Festival for their Beale Street Music Festival in 1990. The festival focus was moved from the historic nightclub district to the riverfront Tom Lee Park. As his responsibilities grew, so did his family.

His first son was born on December 9, 1981 in Memphis. Alexander James Holt became the first grandson in the family. His second son, Andrew Paul Holt, was born June 23, 1983. Lauren Diane Holt was born January 13, 1986, followed by Elizabeth Marie Holt on April 8, 1988. All of the children were born in Memphis.

Also in the 1990, Jim helped originate a Contemporary Christian Music holiday tour promoted by Mid-South Concerts called "The Young Messiah Tour". The tour, which featured an ensemble cast of the top Contemporary Christian artists including Sandy Patty, The Gathiers, Carmen, and Steven Curtis Chapman, played in 10 to 12 cities each year between Thanksgiving and Christmas. The tour played in the nation's largest sporting arenas in major metropolitan cities from the east coast to the west coast. The Young Messiah Tour, which is still regarded as the most successful Christian music tour of all time played to over 500,000 people in 40 cities over its five year run. These concerts were well received by the public, but the artists' demands and the rising cost of arenas caused the series to end after a run of five years.

Jim, Georgia, Alex and Andy with great-grandmother Louise W. Holt in February 1985.

During his fourteen years with Mid-South Concerts, he became involved in booking talent at regional community festivals, such as Riverfest in Little Rock, Jubilee Jam in Jackson, and Dogwood Arts Festival in Knoxville, This festival activity is what led to his desire to become involved with Memphis-in-May.

Jim left Mid-South Concerts in 1993 and formed his own company, Holt Entertainment. He worked primarily with Contemporary Christian artists.

In 1997, an associate in Nashville asked Jim to join him in his management firm, which specialized in Christian music artists.

It seemed like a logical fit, so Jim accepted. Jim's home was still in Memphis, and his kids were in school, so he commuted back and forth for the next ten months.

In May of 1998, he received two telephone calls from business associates who suggested that he apply for the position of executive director of Memphis-in-May, since the position had just been vacated. The organization was struggling, and it was looking for new leadership. There were few positions in Memphis where Jim felt he could apply his talent and past experience, and he welcomed the

119

challenge to make Memphis in May thrive again, so he applied.

Jim was hired to lead the festival on October 8, 1998. His first job was to work with creditors to resolve the enormous debt the organization had accrued. There was a limited staff, as much of the work had been outsourced, so he hired a new team, including Mack Weaver, who became CFO, and Diane Hampton, who went on to become vice president.

Jim's first festival was in May of 1999, and it was so successful that it was the turning

point for Memphis in May. The enormous debt was paid in full and a six-figure sum was still in the bank. The only event that caused considerable worry was a young girl from the honored country, Morocco, had been reported missing. She didn't speak English, and had disappeared. Memphis police and the FBI were alerted, and Jim spent an entire evening without sleep.

When they found her, the girl had made her way to the casinos south of Memphis, where she had been hired as a dancer. She wanted to remain in the USA. She was located and returned to her country's staff. Everyone, including Jim, was greatly relieved.

The pressures of his business and problems with Georgia's health resulted in their separation in 2000 and divorce in 2001.

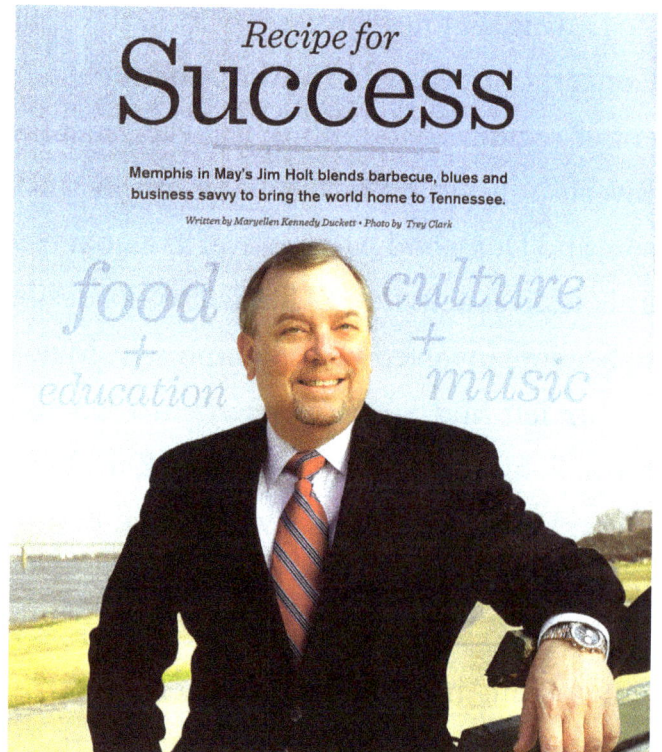

Memphis in May International Festival

Recipe for Success

Memphis in May's Jim Holt blends barbecue, blues and business savvy to bring the world home to Tennessee.

Written by Maryellen Kennedy Duckett • Photo by Trey Clark

food + education + culture + music

Memphis in May headquarters building, located at 56 S. Front St., Memphis, TN 38103.

Jim was made CEO in 2001, then president and CEO in 2002. The organization has grown to over three million dollars in assets, while gaining widespread recognition and respect within the festival industry. The festival has earned 216 prestigious Pinnacle Awards from the International Festival and Events Association.

In 2012, Memphis in May purchased a new permanent home on South Front Street. Its location near the business district and Tom Lee Park, make it an ideal home. It will house the many artifacts and gifts from foreign countries the festival has received through the years.

Posing for a group picture during the welcome reception tendered by Memphis in May Festival executives for Philippine dignitaries at the Brooks Museum of Art are (l-r) MIM President James Holt, Shelby County Mayor Mark Luttrell, Ambassador Jose Cuisia, Memphis City Mayor AC Wharton, and 2012 MIM Chairman of the Board Calvin Anderson.

Liza Holt, with son Gabriel Thomas Holt, born December 6, 2010.

Jim Holt, Board Chair Kristen Wright, Indira Gumarova, Ambassador H.E. Hynek Kmonicek and Mayor Jim Strickland.

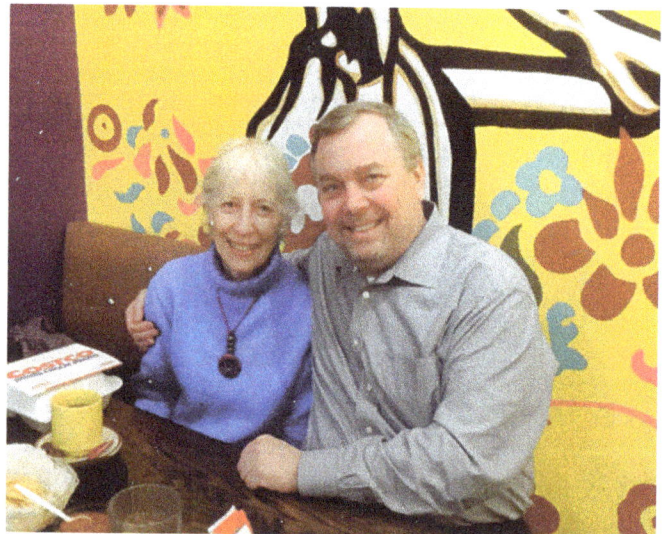

James L. Holt, son of Paul Jr., visits with his Aunt Bobbie Lou Hunt, Paul Jr.'s sister.

The above picture was taken December 14, 2014. Jim had taken his family to Florida for a week-end. From left to right: Liza Holt, Alex Holt, Jim Holt (father), Andy Holt, and Laurie Holt. All enjoyed this trip, so Jim decided to have another weekend tour of Florida.

Jim and his fiance Brooke Tweddell in 2017.

www.ingramcontent.com/pod-product-compliance
Lightning Source LLC
Chambersburg PA
CBHW080802300326
41914CB00055B/1021